THE CRUCIBLE OF CHANGE

The Crucible of Change

THE SOCIAL DYNAMICS OF
PASTORAL PRACTICE

Andrew M. Greeley

SHEED AND WARD: NEW YORK

© *Sheed and Ward, Inc., 1968*

Library of Congress Catalog Number 68-26039

Manufactured in the United States of America

For the Barry's, Jim and Grace Ann,
who were around at the beginning

CONTENTS

Introduction   9

I THE CHURCH AND SOCIETY:
PROBLEMS AND POSSIBILITIES

  1 The Church: Religion and Social Structure   19

  2 The Church and the Personality   32

  3 The Church and the Culture   42

  4 The Church as a Social Organization   52

II THE CHURCH AND COMMUNITY

  5 Community in the Church   69

  6 The Church as Neighborhood   82

  7 The Church as "New Community"   90

  8 The Church as Worship   100

  9 The Church as Diocese   110

III THE CHURCH AND ITS PEOPLE

  10 The Formation of a Christian   127

  11 The Church and Young People   135

  12 The Church and Women   145

7

8   *Contents*

13 The Church and Vocations   *153*

IV *THE CHURCH AND THE FUTURE*
14 The Parish of the Future   *167*
15 Leadership and the Christian Community   *179*

Introduction

There are four contributions which, I trust, a book like the present one may hope to make.

First, it would provide an example of how one might view the pastoral work of the Church from the sociological perspective, and demonstrate both the values and limitations inherent in such a perspective. In my judgment, the most important advantage of the perspective is the one developed in the early chapters of this volume: Sociology helps us to see pastoral work in realistic perspective by demonstrating to us the necessity for modest expectations. It protects us from the twin dangers of naive illusion and naive disillusion.

Secondly, while a book like this will provide no simple answers and no concrete programs, it will at least be an exercise of the sociological imagination speculating about the problems of pastoral work in the contemporary Church, and thus may indicate the general directions in which some pastoral activity could intelligently proceed. For example, we shall speak of the tension between the

Church as a community and the Church as an organization, and of both the problems and the possibilities in the quest for community. What follows from these analyses, if they are valid, is that the Church ought to be much more concerned than it is about the effectiveness of its organizational styles, and both more enthusiastic and more wary about the current quest for community.

Thirdly, the perspective of sociology enables us to ask some probing questions about certain kinds of pastoral activity in which we are presently engaged. In later chapters we will pose a few such questions about liturgy, youth work, and the "New Community." Hopefully, in the face of such questions, there will be a serious reconsideration of certain emphases currently to be observed in pastoral activity.

Fourth, I would hope, at a minimum, that this volume would encourage more skepticism about much that is currently masquerading in the Church today as behavioral science. The pop-psychology and pop-sociology which abound contain many good ideas and many sound suggestions, but there is also much nonsense—some of it pernicious—posing as wisdom, in sentences which begin with either "psychologists tell us," or "sociologists say." When the reader puts down this volume it is my hope that, should he ever encounter such a sentence again, he will ask questions, such as: *Who* are these sociologists? *Where* did their views appear? *Where* is their *evidence?* Until satisfactory answers are given to these questions, polite skepticism is the only intelligent posture.

This book, then, is intended first of all for the pastoral

workers of the Church—priests, sisters, seminarians, and lay people—who are engaged directly in the Church's ministry, full time or part time, as instructors or teachers or in a vast variety of parochial activities. It is also intended for those interested in the evaluation of the efforts of pastoral workers and charged with designing the plans for future pastoral effort, thus including, I would think, not only clergy and religious, but virtually all Catholics seriously concerned about the development of the Church. It is not a "How to do it" book, nor a technical one. It is, rather, a series of reflections on the activity of the Church and its pastoral ministry from the sociological perspective, designed, as said before, more to ask right questions than to provide pat answers.

In the first section of the book, we shall discuss the Church and the system whereby people seek meaning and belonging in contemporary society. Note that the Church is but one such system in contemporary America, though it holds an excellent strategic position. We shall then turn to the limitations of the Church's strategic position, and how they are imposed by the social structure, the human personality, and the prevailing culture. We conclude by inquiring what kind of organizational reevaluation and change is appropriate, given both the opportunities and the problems of the current Church.

In the second section, we shall focus on the critical issues of the quest for community, and on the implications of this quest for the Church as a neighborhood, as a "New Community," as engaged in worship, and as a metropolitan organization.

We shall then consider some of the particular problems the Church encounters in its interaction with the individuals who constitute its people. We will be concerned, first of all, about their training and education, and then about the two classes of people within the Church who are, so often, the victims of discrimination—women and young people.

Finally, we shall summarize the observations of the book by attempting—in a wild, and I fear, quite unsociological burst of prophesy—a vision of the parish of the future.

This book, therefore, is modest in its goals; it intends to present a point of view that is both healthily skeptical and yet open to hopeful experiment, based on realistic assessment of what *is* and, thus, of what may be.

Thou Shalt not answer questionaires
Or Quizzes upon World-Affairs
  Nor with compliance
Take any test. Thou Shalt not sit
With Statisticians nor commit
  A Social science.

W. H. AUDEN*

* Excerpt from "Under Which Lyre" from *Nones* (New York: Random House, 1951), pp. 69-70.

THE CRUCIBLE OF CHANGE

I

THE CHURCH AND SOCIETY: PROBLEMS AND POSSIBILITIES

1 *The Church:*
Religion and Social Structure

In modern Western society it is difficult to conceive of religion existing apart from a church. We occasionally acknowledge that there are "religious" men who do not belong to a church, or are at least not active in ecclesiastical affairs. But religion for us means "organized religion," related to a specific institution and limited to specific social situations. Nevertheless, in most of the societies in which man has lived, religion has been both less institutionalized and more pervasive. Differentiated religious institutions have emerged only in relatively advanced and complex human societies.

There are many sociological explanations for the evolution of religion, but the one that I find most helpful is that of Professor Thomas Luckmann. Luckmann points out that man, unlike other animals, is able to detach himself from immediate experience because he is able to confront his fellowmen humanly, in face-to-face situations. This ability to detach oneself from immediate experience leads to the individuation of consciousness in the formation of a sense of Selfhood. In the very process of forming his Selfhood, his consciousness, man constructs interpretive schemes to explain the world around him and his experience with other human beings. These interpretive schemes, in turn, become systems of meaning. Thus, for Luckmann, the very process of the formation of the self is, in fact, religious: ". . . the transcendence of biological nature by human organisms is a fundamentally religious process"—that is to say, fundamentally a meaning-giving process.*

None of us, of course, goes through such a meaning-giving process in a context isolated from the history and culture of which we are a part. We rather inherit a world view which we then, to a greater or lesser extent, shape to meet our own needs.

Man is naturally religious in that he seeks meaning for his own existence and for the context in which he finds himself. Religion is nothing more than a world view that he acquires partly through inheritance and partly by his own efforts to interpret reality for himself. Luckmann calls this world view "The Invisible Religion" because in complex societies it often has nothing to do either with organized religion or a church. (More frequently, however, it has some contact with both organized religion and a church, although in a way that we may characterize as "folk religion.")

As human society grows more complex and more sophis-

* *The Invisible Religion* (New York: Macmillan, 1967).

ticated, a segment of the world view is differentiated from the whole and is specifically labeled as "sacred." This sacred cosmos, in turn, becomes the concern of a specialized religious institution and of the specialized religious institutional functionaries whose rôle it is to act as custodians of the sacred segment of the world view, the fundamental core of the world view of the whole interpretive system.

As societies grow increasingly complex and dynamic, however, it frequently becomes extremely difficult for the institutional custodian of the world view to keep pace with the forces of change. In the last five centuries of the Western world, when highly specialized institutions emerged to occupy specific areas of human life, institutionalized religion failed to develop its interpretive scheme rapidly enough to provide meaning for total human life. Hence the non-religious institutions developed their own specific systems of meaning which are relevant for their own effort. The church, no longer an institution responsible for the whole of the world view, becomes a specialized institution like all other institutions, with a system of meaning valid for its own sphere, with some validity for other spheres, but lacking universal application.

This development does not mean, however, as observers like Bishop Robinson and Harvey Cox would have us believe, that man has become less religious. It simply means that the church is no longer the only purveyor of meaning, and indeed, no longer the only purveyor of even religious meaning. There are a number of meanings available, some of them specifically sacred and religious, some of them partially sacred and religious, some of them quite secular; and each of these systems of meaning has a greater or lesser connection with the traditional churches which have been the custodians of religious explanation. In Luckmann's view, religious explanations are particularly relevant in those areas of human life where a larger institution—economic, governmental, political—does not provide a functionally determined explanation for human activity.

Religion has therefore become a private matter in which the individual, within the context of his own social-psychological inheritance, experience, and needs, forms (with some guidance from traditional religious institutions) a world-view which gives meaning to the private sphere in his life (which he has come to think is, in fact, *his* life) and also provides some hint for connections between the private sphere and the public sphere. Religious interpretations, some representing the official churches and others clearly not acting on behalf of the church, compete with each other for consumer preference in the marketplace of ideas. Clearly this is a very different relationship between man and religions than the world has known in the past, and it should be emphasized once again that it does not mean that man has become irreligious; it simply means that man's relationship to institutional religion is vastly different from what it has ever been before.

Luckmann concludes his analysis by noting that even if there is a variety in the marketplace of religious ideas, there are certain basic themes of social structure in modern society which have a particularly strong religious appeal and which any system of interpretation must stress if it is to appeal to the "consumer," such as familism, sexuality, individual autonomy, and self-realization.

Such highly individualistic values might be the core of semantic content of "a new social form of religion" in a capitalist society whose original existence depends on individualism and whose continued existence depends on the ritual reaffirmations at least, of the value of autonomy and self-expression. These values are part of the new sacred cosmos of industrial society.

But we think Luckmann has missed an extraordinarily important point as we will stress many times in this volume. Modern man is not happy with the individualism that has made affluence and abundance possible but which has also isolated him from intimate and primordial relationships in most of the areas of his life, has deprived him of organic relationships with the rest of the world, and has provided him with a highly segmented interpretive scheme. In other words, modern man is not very happy with his "new social form of religion;" and the hippies and the psychedelic generation represent a very clear and explicit rejection of this religion, even though their attempt to return to a more organic, coherent, and intimate world view is at least as sick if not sicker than the societies from which they have "cut out."

We are not prepared to say that the churches can, or even should, reassert their old priority and monopoly on religious interpretation. An identification of institutional church with the cosmic world view, it appears to us, was merely a step in the human evolutionary process and one which, to a very considerable extent, made the church dependent on the organized social structure, which it was expected to justify and validate. In the present position of the churches, the open marketplace of religious ideas enables them to play a more dynamic, creative rôle and also to demand from their members a more conscious and explicit acceptance of religious values to which the churches are committed and to which they claim to bear witness.

But in addition, the quest for community which we will describe in several later chapters, represents a yearning for small, meaningful units of fellowship, and hence, in Luckmann's terms, for religious fellowship. Such fellowship not only protects man's humanity in a highly institutionalized society, but it may also provide the basis for man's ultimate re-humanization of the urban, technological structure itself. In other words, to Luckmann's themes of self-expression and autonomy, we can also add the theme of community as one of the most basic in modern man's "new social form of religion." For both ideological and historical reasons, the churches have the best resources to cope with this quest for community, and hence such a quest represents, from a strategic point of view, the church's most useful "point of insertion" in modern society. As we shall assert repeatedly in this volume, the quest for community is, abstractly speaking, neither good nor bad. If it lacks perspective, is divisive, etc., it can be dangerous for the churches; but there does not seem at the present state of the development of man's religious activities any more crucial drive. The churches will either associate themselves with the quest for meaningful community, that is to say, religious community, or they will gradually lose what little strategic location they still have in the open marketplace of world views.

Allowing for the stiff competition the churches must meet squarely within their former preserve, and considering both the innate and acquired characteristics of the confused crowds who eye ecclesial wares with growing indifference or distaste, the pastoral sociologist cannot support anything like great expectations. He can only counsel very modest ones, indeed.

The first finding of social science about pastoral theory and practice is a melancholy one. The social scientist must affirm that despite all efforts, despite the best techniques, *the pastoral worker will have little or no impact on most of his flock most of the time.* This is a hard saying, and one that is ill-designed to win much popularity for the social scientist, particularly in the present condition of American religion.

For example, what we know of the dynamics of the human personality teaches us that the prejudiced person (whether Protestant, Catholic, or Jew) does not acquire his bigotry from his religion and is not likely to shed it through religious influences. All the sermons in the world will not really eliminate the bigotry of a neurotic anti-Semite, nor any other bigotry either, for that matter, since the bigot is essentially a sick person. His narrow and limited perception of the world makes it quite simple for him to "tune-out" any message from his religious leader. True, churches have not preached enough against bigotry, but if anyone thinks that more sermons or more attempts at education are going to eliminate or even notably reduce prejudice and bigotry, then the social scientist is forced to affirm that this is a naive assumption.

It is frequently asserted in the religious press that the time has come for the Church to be relevant to the needs and problems of modern man. It is rarely said just who "modern man" *is,* or what his needs are, though one gets the impression, as one reads between the lines, that "modern man" is the agnostic university student and professor. Nor is it evident how the Church is to be relevant to someone who in principle rejects the very possibility of the relevance of religion to modern life. I do not intend to argue that the Church should not struggle for relevance, but what I know of the dynamics of the human personality and of human society leads me to affirm that the most relevant message imaginable will have only marginal impact on most people to whom it is addressed. A thoroughly modern and relevant version of Christianity might appeal, at the very most, to five or ten per cent more people than currently listen to the Christian message. A realistic appraisal of the prospects for relevance leads us to conclude that there are vast numbers of people who would not even listen to the message, no matter how relevant, and other vast numbers who will listen no matter how irrelevant it might be. Far more important, in the long run, than the relevance of our message is the psychological and sociological equipment which our listeners bring when they come to hear the message. Upon the forces which fashion such equipment, the Church has little in the way of direct or even indirect influence.

The controversy over Catholic education, for example,

betrays an extremely unrealistic expectation of what religious effort is able to accomplish. At the time of the race riots on the southwest side of Chicago, Father Dennis Geaney published an article in *Ave Maria* in which he cited the fact that many young people in the riots wore jackets from Catholic high schools, and he found this a clear proof of the failure of Catholic secondary education. If one expects the schools to eliminate the prejudice of young people whose homes, friendship groups, and neighborhood communities are filled with it, then obviously the schools have failed. Similarly, if one expected Catholic schools to turn out liturgically enthusiastic Christians at precisely the time when no other institution in the American Church was even concerned about liturgy, then the schools indeed have failed. If we are convinced that formal education has the power to turn the overwhelming majority of its students into a species that cannot be found in the home or neighborhood environment, then the Catholic schools, which failed to produce dedicated, socially conscious Catholics, are certainly failures. As a matter of fact, schools which failed to produce saints could be considered failures. But anyone who has paid much attention to the dynamics whereby the human infant or child acquires his values and norms, would have entertained much less exalted, much more realistic expectations. For an institution which does not begin to influence the child until he is six years old, and then only intermittently, can influence only those children for whom there is strong reinforcing influence in the family milieu.

Another manifestation of naive pastoral optimism is the

"magic answer" syndrome. People of this mentality assume that all the Church needs to do is to apply the right technique and it will begin to get marvelous results. The specific technique may vary. It could be a new form of catechetics, the Newman Club, CCD, liturgical participation, group dynamics, "sensitivity" training, pentecostal meetings, cursillos, or almost any device that one would care to mention. The true believer is convinced that if his answer is followed, most if not all of the pastoral problems of the Church will quickly vanish.

The confessors of guilt and the critics of Catholic schools, the devotees of the magic answer, the advocates of push-button Christianity, seem little bothered by the historical evidence that most techniques of preaching the Gospel, including those used by its first Preacher, have been notoriously unsuccessful. It really doesn't seem to matter much that none of the magic answers have worked in the past; somehow or other they are expected to work in the present.

It is interesting to speculate on what precise model of man is postulated in such naive assumptions about pastoral effectiveness. He seems to be almost angelic, without heredity, without environment, without passions, without fears, without needs, without neuroses, without cultural values that he has assimilated from his very earliest days, without patterns of thinking and acting that are almost as unconscious as breathing. He is a *tabula rasa* which can be exposed to a religous experience of some sort, in a school, a group discussion, or a sermon series on prejudice, and develop all the required Christian virtues. If he makes a cursillo or participates in the liturgy or is exposed to the salvation—history catechetics, or hears preaching on racial justice, then this model of man will become the sort of Christian he ought to be: perfect.

About all a social scientist can reply is: "Would to God that it were so!" But if it were, then one suspects the world would have been converted long ago. However, there would have been no need for conversion, because such a model of man is blessedly free of that ancient and ineradicable imperfection of men traditionally known as Original Sin. A man comes into the world with, first, the genetic and biological limitations of his physical inheritance. He quickly acquires the styles and patterns of thought, the attitudes and values, the inclinations, the expectations of behavior which are typical of the culture of which his family is a part. He works out the patterns of relationships with his mother and father, his brothers and sisters, with greater or lesser degree of success, and in the process develops inclinations and propensities which will stay with him for the rest of his life. His intelligence, his emotions, his values, his goals are all profoundly affected and firmly shaped by his family experience, long before his seventh birthday. And the family continues to mold his personality, directly and indirectly, through the internalization of family values, for the rest of his life. His hopes, his fears, his expectations of others, his view of the world, his attitude toward work, and his respect for himself are forged into the patterns of his personality, in many instances long before he even knows there is a church.

None of this is to argue that the Church cannot have an

impact on him, even in the absence of reenforcements from his family or against the wishes of his family, but it is to argue that on the basis of our present knowledge of the dynamics of personality in society, we can expect any religious message to have only limited effect on the human being, and such effect will be strictly within the context already established by other institutions.

Given, therefore, human personality and social systems, a church can expect to have only marginal impact on most people, even with the sophisticated and "relevant" pastoral techniques we now know or with those we are likely to have in the foreseeable future. The vast majority of our audience either are unwilling or unable to listen to what we say, and if we venture forth to battle the forces of wickedness with naive notions of what we can expect from our pastoral techniques and what sort of obstacles in the human personality we are dealing with, our disillusionment will be such that we will very shortly give up the battle. Too many people involved in pastoral work have unrealistic expectations, and when these are shattered, they give up in disgust or despair. They would have been much better advised if they, or those who trained them, had realized how very imperfect the world is, how very imperfect human nature is, and how very imperfect are even the most sophisticated pedagogical or pastoral techniques that we now possess.

None of this is to argue that we should not constantly strive to refine, to renew, to reexamine and reconsider our pastoral efforts. At no time can we honestly say that we could not be doing better, but we must be careful of the meaning we assign to the word "better", because all we can expect from a change of technique is that we will do *a little* better. From the theological viewpoint, this ought to be worth the effort. The pastoral worker ought to be content with pecking away at the proverbial ball of iron. He ought to be content with having marginal impact on a minority. A healthy infusion of Old Testament "saving remnant" theology and the seeming failure of the Lord of the New Testament ought to be sufficient grounds for vigorous effort, even with very modest expectations. The relevant question is not whether our institutions are perfect or even whether they can be perfect. It is, rather, whether they can be improved somewhat, so that we can do a somewhat better job.

Realism and modest expectations do not mean either cynicism or despair. They mean, rather, modest hopes and hard work; he who has modest hopes may not radiate very much starry-eyed enthusiasm, but neither is he likely to give up in the face of discouragement, and on occasion he may even find himself surprised when the returns far exceed his modest expectations.

2 *The Church and the Personality*

The major weakness of the magic answer approach criticized in the last chapter is that those who follow it are so concerned with their own ideas, techniques, and enthusiasm that they have little if any time to look at the people toward whom their pastoral energies are directed. They are very much like college professors who constantly rearrange their curriculum in an effort to find an ever more elegant way of presenting the subject matter, without paying any attention to the personality needs and development of their students, as though the cognitive development of the human personality could be divorced from its general development.

But no technique, no message, no approach, however elegant or consistent or convincing in theory, will have any effect unless it is adjusted to meet the people for whom it is intended *where they are,* in the real world in which they live. If, for example, one informs an adolescent that the catechesis being taught is based on salvation history and is very relevant for his life, he is not thereby going to be impressed unless the salvation history he hears really does meet him where he is, with his needs and problems. The a priori temptation is strong for all human beings, but particularly for religious functionaries and, more particularly, for religious functionaries who are Catholic.

We may very well wish to lead our people to the stars. Any ambition short of this would be unworthy of a pastoral worker. But, to repeat, we shall never lead them to the stars or anywhere else unless we are prepared to start with them where they are, not where they should be, not where we think they ought to be, but where, in fact, we find them.

The most effective pastoral workers have either a conscious or a subconscious sensitivity to the existential situation of their flocks, but unfortunately little has been done to systematize the wisdom that undergirds this sensitivity. Although every human being is different and everyone has his own particular religious *existence,* there are certain patterns of religious attitudes and orientations which can serve as general headings under which a good deal of human religious behavior can be subsumed. Everyone is different, but everyone is also similar to many others. The patterns of similarity can be extraordinarily useful to the one engaged in pastoral work if only because such patterns will give him some idea both of the religious antecedents and of the religious problems of the people with whom he is working.

Unfortunately, from the point of view of an embryonic pastoral sociology, relatively little work has been done on the subject of religious styles. Although Max Weber, the father-founder of contemporary sociology, spoke of the different religious styles of the soldier, the scholar, and the merchant, and his analysis has a certain intrinsic plausibility, little in the way of empirical research has been done to validate his insights, much less to describe other systematic patterns of religious behavior. In this chapter we propose to set out a four-fold typology of such patterns. We make no pretense to producing a definitive classification of religious styles, nor even one that has much empirical validation. It is merely our intention to suggest that this typology of religious styles may be of some use in sorting out the frequently chaotic phenomenon we observe in people's religious life.

The first distinction on which this typology is based is the distinction between *elite* and *folk* religion. *Elite* religion is the religion of the religious scholar, theologian, the ecclesiastical bureaucrat, and the professional religious functionary. It is the religion of the Creeds, the sacred writings, and the ecclesiastical traditions of a religious group, the official religion—that which the leaders of a religious community would use as a measure of orthodoxy. For the Catholic Church, elite religion can be found in the writings of the Fathers, in the theologians, the conciliar documents, the official catechisms, in the teachings of the theology courses in the seminaries and universities, and in the religion text books in grammar school and high school. It is the religion as described in encyclopedic articles about a church. It is that faith the profession of which is taken in theory to mark the authentic believer.

Folk religion, on the other hand, is something quite

different. As Gustave Mensching, the German sociologist, pointed out, the elite religious traditions of the great world religions, for all their scholarly refinement and precision of expression, frequently fail to meet the emotional needs of their members, particularly the less educated members. Thus there evolves a folk religion, a mixture of the elite traditions and various superstitious beliefs and practices which have survived from an earlier stage of religious development.

Such folk religions are particularly obvious, for example, in the case of voodoo in Haiti, a mixture of Christianity and African paganism, or of the *costumbre* in Guatemala, a mixture of ancient Indian nature religion and Spanish Catholicism. But one need not go to Haiti or Guatemala to find folk religion. It may be found, with only slight admixtures of superstitious orientation or practice, in many of the "ordinary" members of the great religious traditions who fashion their folk faith not so much by combining the elite tradition with paganism but by selecting and rearranging doctrines from the elite tradition to fit their own special emotional and religious needs.

For in the elite traditions, certain elements of the creed, practice, and worship have more importance than others. Thus, the doctrine of the Trinity is more important for Catholics than the doctrine of the saints, and similarly the Mass is far more important than Marian devotions. Much of folk Catholicism, particularly in the more highly developed nations, consists of rearranging these hierarchies of value, so that, for example, the religious system of a given person may easily give the veneration of saints and Mary prime importance, while still maintaining a technical orthodoxy.

There is no way of knowing how much folk religion of this sort there is in the Catholic Church, even in the North Atlantic countries, but it seems safe to assume that many, if not most Catholics reveal something of the folk approach in their religious orientation. This is partly because folk tradition has a way of surviving from generation to generation despite the changes and developments in the elite tradition, and partly because, given the somewhat aloof and reserved format of Catholic creed and cult before the second Vatican Council, the folk style met emotional needs which elite Catholicism generally did not meet.

The second distinction, based on the work of Gordon Allport, is the difference between the *instrumental* and the *non-instrumental* approach to religion. Fascinated by the fact that there seemed to be a positive correlation between religiousness and prejudice, Allport asked himself through a long series of studies whether there are certain kinds of religious styles that are more conducive to prejudice than others. He then developed a measure of religious orientation which purported to identify an *instrumental* approach to religion. People who scored high on this measure tended to *use* religion; they viewed religious practice as a means of preserving peace of mind, of protecting order in the world, of providing answers to basic questions that they say beset them, of achieving certainty and serenity in their activities and respectability in their social class. Those who scored low on the measure of instrumentalism, on the other hand, tended to view religion not as something to be used for other goals, but rather as a means of opening out one's personality toward other human beings and toward God.

Non-instrumental religion, then, is religion oriented less toward the meeting of emotional needs for security and reassurance than toward meeting one's need to render altruistic service and to worship. Allport found, as we might expect, that when the religious people were divided into these two groups, the instrumentally religious were more prejudiced than the *non*-religious, whereas the non-instrumentally religious were considerably less prejudiced, in turn, than the non-religious. This distinction between the two modes of religious behavior—one involving a cognitive style with narrowed perception and increased prejudice, and the other involving a cognitive style with broadened perception and decreased prejudice—has been overlooked in many of the studies claiming to establish a direct correlation between religiousness and bigotry.

If these two distinctions in religious behavior are cross-tabulated, four different modalities appear: the folk-instrumental religious style, the folk-non-instrumental, the elite-instrumental, and the elite-non-instrumental.

The first of the four styles we might call the *magical*—those believers whose patterns of religious orientation and behavior are simultaneously folk and instrumental. These not only select those items from the religious faith which are appropriate for their own emotional needs, but also select precisely those items which are most likely to *produce results*. They vigorously and enthusiastically profess their faith in teachings which are essential for their own reassurance and certainty, regardless of how important they might be in any elite presentation of the propositions of the faith. They also engage in precisely those forms of cultic action which seem most likely to get immediate results. Special devotions, private revelations, cult, mystical phenomena, sure-fire methods of prayer, and vigorous insistence on the importance of sexual morality and certain specified items of religious practice (Mass on Sunday and, until the recent abrogation, no meat on Friday)—these constitute the staples of their religious activity, which may be pursued with a great deal of rigor, enthusiasm and devotion, but with little regard for the broader social and ethical concerns of the religious faith.

The folk non-instrumental religious style is that which is often attributed to saints like the Curé D'Ars or the legendary Breton or Irish peasant woman. These people know, or are alleged to know, very little theology; they read few books, have no notion of what may have transpired at the Councils of the Church, and they engage in exercises of piety which would be embarrassing to their more sophisticated coreligionists. Nonetheless, the depth and sincerity of the non-instrumental religious style is such that their lives are frequently wonders of piety and even sanctity. Their knowledge and devotion may be narrow, but it is deep; their charity may not be based on social encyclicals or knowledge of existentialist theology, but it is nonetheless remarkably effective. The only problem with this religious style is that, despite the great praise it receives, particularly from those of anti-intellectual tendency, it does not seem, in fact, to be very common.

The third religious style is that of the elite-instrumentalist, who knows rather clearly the principal propositions of his faith and understands rather well which cultic and ethical practices are most important, but whose religion is oriented essentially toward the satisfaction of his need for security, stability, and reassurance. This well-informed religious instrumentalist can be found almost anywhere on the liberal-conservative continuum. He may be a clericalist or an anti-clericalist, a "two dollar a Sunday" Catholic, or a daily communicant, a racist or an integrationist. The important point about him is that his religious behavior has about it a certain rigidity, narrowness and inflexibility. However high-principled and devout he may be, tolerance is only rarely found in his behavior. To be tolerant, one must face at least the possibility that someone else may be right; but this the instrumental religionist is quite incapable of doing.

The fourth and final style in our typology is that of the elite-non-instrumental group—those who are well informed on the hierarchy of religious values within their group, and whose faith and behavior open them up to the world in which they live and to their fellowmen whom they wish to serve. They are at least the raw material out of which the dedicated religionist presumably can be shaped and whose personality configurations and religious orientation make them most readily disposed to respond to pastoral effort with the kind of response that the pastoral worker presumably expects.

This typology, obviously, is very sketchy and general. Much more research would have to be done before its use as a tool for understanding would be really satisfactory. However, it does indicate that the religious activity we witness around us can have many varied sources deep in the personality, and is often shaped to meet many emotional needs. Few, if any of us, choose our religious style. It results rather from the experiences of our childhood, from the social class in which we were reared, from our education, and from the experiences we have undergone during the crises of adolescence and early adulthood. Our attitudes toward God and toward the Church are profoundly influenced by these styles, which in their turn were profoundly influenced by our relationship with our parents. It is easy for one's unconscious to confuse God with one's father and the Church with one's mother, and perhaps nothing is more important in shaping the religious styles of a person as he grows up than the parental relationship. The religious style is changed only with very great difficulty, and the distance from a folk-instrumental attitude toward religion, to an elite-non-instrumental attitude is one that very few people are likely to traverse.

It will take many years to eliminate the distrust, suspicion, and fear which characterize relationships between men and women, between parents and children, or to eliminate the kinds of childhood experiences which lead to an instrumental attitude toward religion. And it may take long years of refinement in the arts of catechetics and homiletics before elite religious attitudes become even intelligible to large numbers of people. In the meantime, the ignorance and the weakness which is the lot of man, will provide a context of severe limitation for all pastoral effort. What must be insisted upon is this: *the Church is not directly responsible for the religious styles of its members,* although, of course, to the extent that the Church fails to live up to its own principles, it does slow down the progress of the human race toward trust and love and, thus, toward the kinds of religious behavior which such attitudes produce.

But in the short run, the pastoral worker must resign himself to the fact that, for most of the people in three of the four typologies we have mentioned, he can do little more than fulfil certain specified religious needs. The folk-instrumental religionist does not really want a priest or a minister; he wants a witch doctor. The folk-non-instrumental religionist is in communion with God, with nature and with his fellowmen, but tends to go his own way, and while he may be tolerant of the efforts of the pastoral worker, he feels no need for such help to deepen or enrich his piety.

The elite-instrumental religionist will beset, harass, and harangue the pastoral worker, but his intolerance, rigidity, and inflexibility will interfere in developing the kind of religious activity which the pastoral worker thinks desirable.

Thus only those whose religious style seems to be simultaneously elite and non-instrumental are likely to respond to the efforts of the pastoral worker, no matter how great these may be. It is, therefore, with this group that the most effective work can be done, and only here that the pastoral worker can reasonably expect results resembling those his religious commitment deems desirable.

3 The Church and the Culture

In the previous chapter we pointed out that the expectations of success in pastoral effort are severely limited by the religious styles of the members of any given group. Only one type of the four religious typologies we developed could be considered disposed by personality for genuinely pastoral effort. Another series of limitations derives not so much from the personalities of the people with whom the pastor works, but rather from the general cultural values which are likely to affect pastor and people alike. There may very well be certain elements in American culture which are conducive to religious effort, but as in every other culture the world has ever known, there are values and features of American society which constrain even the most sophisticated religious effort. Let us look at some of them, if only briefly.

1. Above all, Americans are "a people of plenty." From almost the very beginning the American people have believed in the possibility of almost limitless progress in their society. In more recent years this faith in progress has been

reenforced by the almost overwhelming affluence which most Americans enjoy. Even though, at least in theory, the Churches and religious groups have gone through their manichaean phase and are now willing to admit that material and technical progress is a good thing, it is still very difficult for Christianity to feel at ease in a situation where poverty is not only not a virtue but even something against which "war" is to be waged; where frugality is no longer praiseworthy because it interferes with the all-important goal of expanding the Gross National Product. Even if one concedes that the Christian must seek his salvation by effort in this world, and even supposing that the world's values are Christian values, it is difficult to escape the Gospel insistence that the Lord's Kingdom is *not* of this world, and that "treasures should be laid up where the moth and the rust do not consume." Plainly, the Christian must live in a tension between due respect for the good things of this life and expectations and hopes of even better things in the life to come; yet never before in our country's experience has the vast majority of any nation enjoyed our current level of material prosperity, a level which would have seemed rather heavenly to most of our ancestors. Material abundance can hardly be condemned by the Christian, but it does pose a problem for the pastoral worker who, no matter how contemporary his theology, must still face the fact that to be poor even "in spirit" is a bit difficult to manage in a society whose Gross National Product is moving toward a thousand billion dollars a year!

2. American culture is increasingly becoming the culture of the "technique;" so vast and complicated has be-

come the mechanism of what John Kenneth Galbraith calls "the new industrial state" that no single man can hope to understand, not indeed the whole of society, but even the whole of any single important corporate structure. The need for complex planning, information gathering, and technology is both the cause and effect of a knowledge revolution, which in its turn has produced the new man of modern society—the professional expert—the man who is a master at integrating his own complex technical skills with equally complex technical skills of others to produce our relatively smooth-running corporate bureaucracy.

What, indeed, does the Gospel mean to a systems analyst or to a computer programmer? While it should be possible to speak of religion to the new professional, no one seems quite certain yet how this ought to be done. From its past experience, the Church knows how to communicate with scholars and soldiers, with kings and merchants, with peasants and workers; but the denizen of the techno-structure is quite another creature.

3. Modern American culture is essentially urban and metropolitan, and the values of the churches have until very recently been heavily rural and peasant. The intense and sometimes frantic commitment to the problems of the inner city (where, we are told, the action is) seems to be an attempt on the part of the churches to recapture, at least in one segment of society, the kind of community influence it had in the peasant villages of the past. But the attempt is not an altogether successful one, and perhaps, in the final analysis, not really relevant, because modern so-

ciety is not being shaped in the inner city (though conceivably it could be destroyed there). Society is being shaped rather in the professional suburbs where the Church, as Gibson Winter has pointed out, is in a curious kind of thralldom, and in the technical structure "downtown," where the Church is absent and which the Church does not even begin to understand. It may be possible, as we will note in a later chapter, to develop some kind of quasi-*gemeinschaft* community in the suburbs or in the older neighborhoods of the central city, but such communities, far from having significant impact on the crucial problems of modern society, are in fact quite irrelevant to these problems.

4. The Christian churches were formed and reached their maturity in a world where most human contact was face-to-face. But, increasingly for five centuries now, the printing press has interposed the page of a book or a newspaper, both as bridge and barrier, in place of direct human interaction. The recent abandonment of the *Index* would suggest that the Catholic Church has finally come to terms, at least, with the printing press, and this precisely when, if Marshall McLuhan is correct, the printed word is becoming decreasingly important as a means of communication. One need not agree with McLuhan, and one may be very skeptical about the allegedly pervasive influence of the picture tube in the living room. Still the situation in which the whole world can, in fact, come into the home, (even, if one can afford it, in living color) is a new and disturbing situation for the pastoral worker. It is difficult enough to compete with *Star Trek,* or with Bill Cosby; but how does

one compete with Bart Starr or the Viet Cong at supper time?

5. We live in the world of the jet set and the expressway generation, a world where, as Barbara Ward has pointed out, the whole planet has been reduced to a village, around which one can travel now in three hours. But it is a village with three billion people. The Church which has only recently made the transition, with some success, from the farming community of nineteenth century Europe to the urban neighborhood of twentieth century America, now must face the fact that the whole world is part of one's neighborhood and that, in something more than theological theory, every man is one's neighbor. The awesome implications of the shrinking of the globe to a neighborhood have only begun to dawn on both the theorists and the practitioners of pastoral work.

6. The educational level of American Catholics has risen dramatically. The problem this fact presents was typified for the author on a tour of a university parish conducted by its pastor, a good and zealous priest, who was quite at a loss as to how to cope with the university people in his parish, or with the poor Negroes whom the university community tolerated on its fringes. He assured those of us who were on the tour, however, that the backbone of his parish was not the Ph.D.'s and the Ph.D. candidates, but rather the "cap and sweater" people. The tragedy of that particular parish was that the "cap and sweater" people, such as they were, were fast disappearing, and the Negro proletariat and the intellectual aristocracy were both the main support and also the main challenge of the parish.

The Catholic Church did not lose the American working class because it was agile enough to move from the farms and shops of Europe to the factory neighborhoods of America. But whether it is agile enough to meet the situation where, in place of a handful of well-educated people in the parish, the majority of American Catholics now go to college, is another question. In fact, this is the first time in the history of religion that higher education is to be presumed for most of the people pastoral work would reach. The truism, of course, is that the pastor is no longer the universally acknowledged social and intellectual leader of his parish, although not all pastors, by any means, have acknowledged this deterioration of their status. But what *are* the appropriate apostolic and pastoral ventures in a community of well-educated people, particularly when these people are young, and have grave reservations about all the concerns of the organized Church, even though these are concerns which middle-aged liberals find terribly important?

7. It is another truism that contemporary society is highly mobile. Americans are on the move. Perhaps as many as ten per cent of them move every year, and it is a rare person, particularly in the professional and academic elite, who plans to stay in any one community or any one city for a long period of time. But the implicit model of most pastoral behavior has been the parishioner who rarely, if ever, leaves his parish. Whether any kind of depth and intimacy can ever develop in a relationship between the pastor and people in a world on the move, seems highly questionable But if there is no depth and intimacy, how can the pastor expect to lead his flock?

8. Not only do people move rapidly, so do situations. The American culture not only changes, but it is the first culture in the history of the human race in which change is a component of the system; where every moment must mean transition, and where the solution to yesterday's problems are as irrelevant as the questions of the day before. By the time a problem is analyzed and various solutions are tested, it frequently seems that the rapid surge of events has eliminated the need or the possibility of an answer. The Churches, particularly the Catholic Church, are used to moving slowly. Indeed, most large corporate structures move slowly. But the world in which men live moves rapidly and the pastoral worker is often forced to the conclusion that no matter how quick or agile he may be, he is always several steps behind in even grasping the problems his people must face.

9. It is, we are told, a world of science rather than myth, though one is permitted to be skeptical of how correct Bultmann was when he thought that the mere presence of science in modern society did away with man's predilection for myths, not to say superstitions. It is, we are told, a world of the secular rather than the sacred, though one may be permitted to be skeptical of Harvey Cox's claim that the secular is now replacing the sacred. Man has demonstrated in the past a remarkable ability to combine highly contradictory orientations in his personality, and there is no reason to believe that he cannot combine scientism with mythology, and secularism with reverence for the sacred. Nonetheless, some moderns, particularly in the academic and university worlds, are persuaded that the

myth and the sacred are no longer relevant in an age of secular science, and the pastor must attempt either to persuade them of the error of this basic assumption or to communicate with them on religious matters in the rhetoric and vocabulary of secular science. Most of the attempts to do so have not been very convincing to the secularists or to the scientists, nor particularly reassuring to those who are committed to at least a minimal preservation of traditional orthodoxy. There have been many false starts in the dialogue between religion and science, but at least thus far, rather little in the way of meaningful communication.

10. It is not yet clear from empirical data whether the alleged sexual revolution is a figment of the imagination of journalists and very superficial social researchers, though a plausible explanation would be that working-class and peasant sexual mores have infiltrated the middle class, while middle class notions of romantic love seem to have permeated the rest of society. The more relevant problems of the pastoral work of the Christian churches is to find a way of integrating into their world view the positive attitude toward sexual love which has become so much a part of modern culture, while at the same time not conceding to neo-pagans the principle that healthy sex need observe no moral restrictions. It is curious that those disciples of popularized Freud who are all too ready to insist on the healthy and liberating dimensions of sex, overlook the wisdom of the master on its demonic features. True, the churches have not lost sight of the demonic in sex, but neither have they developed in any great detail the early

Christian insight on the positive and personal values of sex. It is no exaggeration to say that the pastoral effort which is unable to do so can have little hope of success in the modern world.

The basic theme running through these comments on the cultural limitations of the pastoral effort is that the churches and their pastors find themselves working in a world which they do not understand, and whose values, norms and behavior are considerably at variance, and in some cases, in direct opposition to the traditional values and norms of Christianity. What is acceptable in modern culture, what can be tolerated, and what must be condemned by prophetic witness-bearing are not at all clear. All cultures impose their own limitations on the effectiveness of pastoral work. But modern American culture presents a special problem, because the churches, by and large, do not understand it, and do not know to what extent they can accept or reject it. The temptation, therefore, is to embrace it without reservation, or, alternately, to reject it without distinction. The pastor who bases his religious efforts on either of these extremes is foredoomed to failure, but he who tries to steer a middle course will find that the charts currently available are of very little help.

In this and the preceding chapters we have taken an extremely cautious view of the expectations the pastoral worker should entertain for the success of his work. We have maintained that the cultural, social, and personality systems impose strict limitations on the degree of effectiveness he can reasonably expect. And we insist once again that while this may be stark realism, it is not despair. If there is much that we cannot expect to accomplish, there are many things that we can, with some reasonableness, hope to achieve. For Christians, at least, the fact that even the Lord's work was only moderately successful (or, from certain perspectives, a rather notorious failure, as stated before), ought to be somewhat reassuring when they tally successes against failures. If there is still a long way to travel, it is at least time to start. And he who knows the length of the journey before he starts is less likely to give up than he who thinks it will be a brief and balmy stroll.

4 The Church
as a Social Organization

If there is one thing that is clear in contemporary writing about the Catholic Church, it is the insistence that it is a community and a people. Indeed, most of us have heard this so often in recent years, that we are probably tired of hearing it. (But it ought to be noted that the communitarian nature of the Church is still stressed far more in theory than in practice.) Frequently, especially in amateur theologizing and sociologizing about the Church, one would gain the impression that the Church as a community is somehow opposed to the Church as a structure (or institution), as though the ideal would be to have a Christian community without structure. It rarely occurs to such commentators that a community without structure is a nonexistent community, because all human groups, even the most simple, quickly evolve established patterns of behavior and agreed-upon norms to regulate these patterns of behavior. In other words, even the most elementary com-

munity has structure and laws. Those who wish to eliminate laws and organization in the Church, and replace
them with affection and love, show little understanding of
man or of society.

I have been assured on occasion that if the Church were
a society like other human societies, it would not be a sign
of God's intervention in history, that in order to be a sign
of such divine intervention, the Church must be a society
that cannot be compared to other human groups. This, of
course, would render any attempt to evaluate the Church's
activities from the point of view of the theory of social
organization pointless and frustrating. Those who accept
such a premise, whether they be new breed or old breed,
simply shrug their shoulders and observe, "But the Church
isn't a human society—it's something divine." The sociologist, under such circumstances, is forced to reply: "For
a society that isn't a human society, the Church surely be-
haves remarkably like one, and has so behaved for over
nineteen hundred years." The sociologist is also forced to
remark, from the perspective of his theological innocence,
that to say the Church cannot be divine if it is a human
society is rather like saying that Christ cannot be divine
because He has a human nature. Indeed, the sociologist
might even say that the very humanness of the Church as a
society might very well be both a stumbling block and
folly (in Pauline Terms) to such simplism, verging on
Docetism.

Frequently, too, it has seemed to me that a kind of theological Hobbesianism can be observed in some commen-
taries on the contemporary Church. One has the

impression from such writings that organization and administration are bad things—that they stunt human spontaneity and freedom, interfere with human love, and frustrate the growth of the human spirit. The social scientist is tempted to marvel at such a view of organization and administration, since it seems to imply that mankind has made no progress in the understanding of social organization since the death of Thomas Hobbes. As both Aristotle and contemporary behavioral scientists realize, administration, organization, and even regulation exist to promote the freedom of the human spirit, not to prohibit it; and several scholarly disciplines, as well as a vast amount of existing empirical research, suggest how the Iron Law of Oligarchy (according to which, organizations always frustrate the ends for which they were brought into being) can be inhibited. If the Church is not a human organization, then the scholarship of the behavioral sciences can be ignored. But if it is, it would be singularly inappropiate for Catholicism not to pay some attention, at least, to what social organizational research has to say about its internal renewal.

Assuming, therefore, that at least some kind of analogical comparison of the Church to other human organizations is still theologically valid, I contend that the problem with the Church is not, as Monsignor Ivan Illitch has suggested, that it has too much organization, but rather that it does not have *good enough* organization, and in many instances, that it simply does not have enough organization. I would go so far as to argue that in many respects the progress of renewal within Roman Catholicism will not be successful unless new and more efficient organization is generated; the appearance of both the Episcopal Synod and the National Hierarchies suggests that this is precisely what is going on. Furthermore, I would contend that supernaturalists like Monsignor Illitch notwithstanding, these new organizations are much more likely to facilitate renewal of the Church if they are advised and assisted by competent experts rather than by untrained visionaries, however charismatic.

In discussing the Church and its organizational aspect, my point of view is not that of a priest, or even a Catholic; I intend to take a hard and critical look at the current organization of the Catholic Church *as a sociologist,* or, as impartially as, let us say, an agnostic student of complex organizations might view the Church. This will enable me to speak with a frankness that might not be possible if I were afraid of treading on ecclesiastical toes. I shall confine myself to eleven statements, each briefly amplified.

1. *The Catholic Church in the world and in the United States has virtually no institution dedicated to research and planning.* There is probably no other large organization in the modern world that has less idea of what it is doing, how much it is accomplishing, or where it is going, than does the Catholic Church. Its social research is, by and large, limited to the gathering of statistics (rather sketchy), and to provide *ad hoc* answers to specific questions, usually as cheaply as possible. Scholars—social, historical, and theological—who could provide the raw material for research and policy-planning are frequently, indeed generally, viewed not with the respect and enthusiasm

most large organizations have for their idea men, but with skepticism and suspicion. Information-gathering, which presumably is the absolute requisite for enlightened and intelligent decision-making, proceeds according to the most primitive and unreliable methods, and the policy-planning function which most complex modern organizations view as absolutely essential, hardly exists in the Catholic Church. Of course, if one contends that the Church need not adjust as the world around it changes, and that the work of the Church remains basically simple even though society grows ever more complex, there is precious little need for research or policy-planning. The establishment of whatever long-range goals are thought necessary can be effectively carried on (presumably) by Ecumenical Councils. However, in the wake of the Vatican Council, such an approach to research and planning within the Catholic Church simply does not appear to be tenable.

2. *It is not clear that the current methods of selecting leadership elites within the Church have produced the most competent or able administrators.* Unquestionably some ecclesiastical leaders are very able, and equally unquestionably, some are incompetent. But any casual reader of the history of the American Church, or even the daily press, cannot escape the conclusion that Church leaders who lack striking ability are found in considerably higher percentage than are less able leaders in most other modern organizations. It also would seem that a considerable amount of administrative talent as well as policy-planning ability is overlooked in the Church because the people

possessing this ability are not considered conservative enough to be "safe." But most research on social organization suggests that at least in the modern world, conservative leadership and "safe" leadership are not the same thing, and that in the long run the goals of an organization are best served by leadership that, while exercising proper precautions, is enlightened enough and progressive enough to create a sense of dynamic movement within the organization. The lack of a system of merit promotion within the Church, as well as the absence of a rigorous search for progressive and dynamic leadership, must be listed as major organizational weaknesses of contemporary Catholicism.

3. An astute observer of contemporary society has made the following comment:

> The dignity of the human person requires the right to act freely and responsibly. For this reason, in social relations, man should exercise his rights, fulfill his obligations and in countless forms of collaboration with others act chiefly on his own responsibility and initiative. This is to be done in such a way that each one acts on his own decision, of set purpose and from a consciousness of his obligation, without being moved by force of pressure brought to bear on him externally.
>
> Where any human society is established on relations of force, it must be regarded as inhuman inasmuch as the personality of its members is repressed or restricted, when in fact they should be provided with

appropriate incentive and means for developing and perfecting themselves.

It's worth noting that the author of this statement is not a specialist in social organization. Nor is he a dreamy social radical. Rather, the principle of *professionalism* in the above paragraph was enunciated by Pope John XXIII in his Encyclical letter *Pacem in Terris,* Article 34. *The dispassionate student of contemporary Catholicism, however, is forced to note that there is not nearly enough professional initiative and responsibility within the Catholic Church.* The feudal relationships, for example, between pastor and curate, or between the religious superior and subject, far from maximizing initiative and responsibility, seem rather to minimize it. In addition to violating what John XXIII would consider a basic human right, this absence of freedom of initiative and responsibility severely inhibits the efficiency of the Catholic Church. For only when men are free to exercise their initiative and to act on their own responsibility do they become capable of making the most intensive and constructive contributions to work in organizations to which they belong. The feudal relationships that continue between superior and subject (even the terms are unfortunate) within the Church are, one might almost say, worse than immoral. They are wasteful. One is further tempted to say that in the complexity of modern society, only an organization which is preserved from complete disaster by the Holy Spirit could have survived such unconscionable waste.

4. *Whatever theoretical advances may have been made*

recently in our understanding of the nature of the Church as a collegial organization, it is difficult to observe very much of this collegiality operating in practice. From a social organizational point of view, collegiality is necessary, not so much on moral grounds, but on sheer pragmatic grounds of efficiency. In an organization composed of educated, competent, and dedicated professionals, modern organizational theory holds that the collegial form of governance is easily the most effective. The collegial leader is occupied not so much with providing answers, but with asking the right questions of the right people; and he does not feel that his authority is weakened in the slightest because decisions are made after consultation and consensus, rather than before.

Thus, for example, John Kennedy did not lose any of his power or effectiveness as a leader because his decision and response to the Cuban missile crisis was the result of a collegial rather than a unilateral decision. Neither, interestingly enough, was the power of the council of ministers of the Soviet Union at all weakened by the fact that their response to Kennedy's response was also, it would seem, collegial. For important matters in modern society, collegial decision-making is no longer optional; yet it would seem that in the face of this almost overwhelming fact, substantial portions of the leadership element within the Catholic Church are not persuaded that collegiality does not threaten their authority. From the viewpoint of social theory, it seems safe to say, the Catholic Church will not even begin to *be* in the modern world until it becomes far more collegial in its day-to-day operations. Unilateral paternalism may be an efficient way to run a Teutonic tribe, or perhaps even a naval ship in combat (though even this is not clear), but it is certainly not efficient for a complex modern organization.

5. *The Catholic Church not only does not have agencies for internal criticism, but, by and large, it does not seem to encourage the existence of such agencies,* even though more recently and independently, the press in the United States has begun to play such a rôle, quite without special invitation. Almost any efficient modern corporation has at least one, and usually several organs of criticism, either internally financed and staffed or provided by some outside agency.

The role of such agencies is to constantly supervise and question the techniques and methodology of the organization. The profession of management consultant has become a complex and elaborate one with many varieties of specialization. The modern organization argues that only when it is constantly being criticized and evaluated in an objective and impartial fashion can it be sure that its responses to the challenges of the world outside are all that they might be. As Kenneth Keniston has recently noted, democratic societies cannot be confident of survival unless the universities within these societies are free to play to the fullest the rôle of social critic. The Catholic universities both in this country and the world have not been, generally speaking, encouraged to be critical, and institutions set up deliberately to carry on evaluation assignments simply do not exist. The dispassionate outside observer would almost be forced to conclude that the Catholic

Church does not feel that it needs internal criticism because it does not feel that it is capable of making any serious mistakes.

6. *Unlike the very considerable number of international organizations both public and private that have emerged in the last quarter of a century, the Catholic Church does not, save in a token fashion, recruit its administrative personnel internationally.* One need not intend any criticism of the Italian people, the Italian clergy, or the Italian hierarchy, to say that it is dysfunctional for morale, and for the effective operation of the Catholic Church to perpetuate the overwhelmingly Italian composition of its professional international leadership. An organization which has international problems must recognize that the canons of efficiency, if not of equity, demand that its personnel also be international. Such internationalization of personnel in the past, of course, was impossible due to problems of transportation and communication, but surely in an age of transoceanic-telephonic communication and supersonic jet transports, such reasons no longer obtain. Even though one hears frequently of the proposed internationalization of the Roman Curia, it must be noted that such internationalization seems to be proceeding much too slowly.

7. *Any effective and efficient modern organization realizes that it must provide responsibility for its personnel at as early an age as possible, and must include at least some relatively youthful personnel at the very highest level of leadership.* It goes without saying, of course, that even if the pastorate in its present canonical form were to be con-

tinued, the thirty-year wait for such a position of responsibility which most American priests, at least, must endure,
is fantastically inefficient. Furthermore, the dispassionate
student of social organization must say that the Catholic
Church fails to promote its most promising people to top
level positions of responsibility at an early enough age.
The problems in the environment which the Church faces,
indeed which any modern organization faces, change so
rapidly that the flexibility necessary to respond demands at
least some youthful leadership. Thus the nineteenth century policy whereby men in their early thirties became
bishops (Gibbons, Ireland, Keane, and Spalding, for example) in their thirties, and archbishops in their early
forties seemed to be a much more efficient way of assuring
dynamic leadership than the present policy. It is interesting to note that, with one exception, none of the members
of the 1960 Kennedy cabinet were old enough to be major
leaders in the American Catholic Church or, indeed, to
have top-level positions in the Roman curia. Granted the
wisdom which comes with age and experience, the complete absence of youthful personnel at the top leadership
level is an extraordinarily inefficient mode of operation.
Similarly, although there are beginnings here and there,
one has to observe that the absence of any truly effective
retirement policy would be incredible in any other complex organization. Only an organization protected by the
Holy Spirit could survive leadership that is (with all reverence) so physically antiquated.

8. *Even though the documents of the Vatican Council
placed emphasis on the need for consultation and commu-*

nication between the leadership elements and the rank and file, there is little evidence that organs to facilitate such communication have come into existence. One has the impression that the general feeling is that such communication and consultation is useful and good, but that it can be approached at a somewhat leisurely pace. However, other modern organizations (including, one might note, military establishments of the various great powers) are convinced that consultation and communication are not optional but absolutely imperative; they expend considerable time and resources in assuring themselves that their channels of communication are as functional as possible. The principle of the human-relations approach to management that holds "Everyone whose cooperation is essential to the implementation of a decision should be seriously consulted about the making of that decision" is not, it should be noted, intended as an ethical principle but as a pragmatic norm for effective behavior.

9. The financial officers of banks who deal intensively with dioceses and religious communities usually have a vast repertoire of stories (most of them funny and some of them tragic) about the financial naiveté and incompetency of some religious leaders. Unquestionably, many church leaders are extraordinarily skillful in matters of finance, but recent public revelations also demonstrate that a fair number are naive and incompetent. The major problem is that *no one can say for sure, regarding Church financial matters, how much incompetency and how much competency there is, in the absence of a careful and standardized routine of fiscal supervision.* The financial procedures and

policies of the Catholic Church are complete mysteries to everyone outside it, and to most of those inside. Indeed, many observers have come to suspect that they are mysteries even to most of those who presumably exercise official financial control. A system of accounting and account ability, not only to prevent disasters of the sort that recently reached the public press, but also to provide the immense savings that standardized financial practices make possible, is absolutely imperative in the Catholic Church. It is also extremely unlikely that a system of accountability can be devised which would not involve, in some way, public accountability.

10. Studies of the efficient operation of bureaucratic structures strongly suggest that in the absence of personal security, most professional staff members cannot operate efficiently, and furthermore, that those who must deal at least intermittently with professional bureaucracies cannot do so effectively unless there is some means by which they may appeal the arbitrary decisions that might be imposed upon them. Thus, *the welfare of both the professional and religious functionaries, as well as of the rank and file members of the Church, and (from the social organizational viewpoint, more importantly) the efficient operation of the organization demand that there be effective protection of the right of appeal*—a protection which generally would include the right of cross-examination, advice by counsel, security from anonymous denunciations, and publication of decisions and of the reasons on which decisions are based. It would be an exaggeration to say that there is no right of appeal in the Catholic Church, but the impression

that a dispassionate outside observer would have is that
few, if any, of the professional personnel in the Church
believe that they will receive fair treatment from such
appellate processes. Once again we must insist that emphasis here is placed on the necessity of the right of appeal, not
so much on ethical grounds as on the purely pragmatic
grounds of what is required for the efficient operation of a
large organization in the complexities of contemporary
life.

11. Finally, *the outside observer would lament the lack
of sophisticated and competent public relations institutions within the Church.* He would think that such inefficiency was particularly dysfunctional at a time when the
Church, with little effort of its own, is receiving a huge
amount of publicity. Such publicity could quite readily
enhance the image of the Church greatly in the mind of
the non-Catholic public, but frequently, because of its
inept public relations procedures, the Church is harmed
by it rather than benefitted. An organization protected by
the Holy Spirit can perhaps escape disaster, at least ultimate disaster, if it cares little or nothing about what
others think of it, but one doubts very much if the Holy
Spirit more than tolerates inept public relations.

This chapter has emphasized the social, organizational
weaknesses of the Catholic Church—the policies and practices that inhibit its efficient and effective functioning in
the modern world. We do not, of course, even imply that
there is malice or bad will behind the policies and practices under discussion. Nor do we intend to deny that in
almost every area we have mentioned some action has al-

ready been taken and some progress is being made. None-theless, it seems to us that our friend, the dispassionate outside observer, would simply not be able to understand why the action has been so hesitant and the progress so slow. And perhaps many Catholics who are strongly dis-affected with the "institutional" Church, quite aware that it needs to have organization, have simply despaired of any but the most radical kind of action as a means toward reorganizing *soon enough and profoundly enough* to avert irrelevance in a world where change is proceeding with inexorable *geometric* progression.

II
THE CHURCH AND COMMUNITY

5 Community in the Church

As we have already indicated, there is no more magic word in the contemporary Church than "community." The priest, we are told, is the maker of the "community," and the community he makes is the Church, or at least the Church must be "in the community." The Christian parish must become a community; man is on a quest for community; community is a goal of renewal. We must create community with our fellowmen. Religious orders must be "communities" once more. The priest and people must strive for community among themselves. Bishops must dialogue with the community of the faithful.

Like many another popular word, "community" has stopped being an aid to rational discourse and has become a slogan. It has ceased to convey meaning, and is now a cliché. Moreover, many of the uses to which it is put are incorrect, and some are absurd. The meaning of the word as found in the statement above is based on the sociological tradition formed by the great European sociologists of the nineteenth century, such as Tonnies, Durkheim, Weber,

Leplay, de Tocqueville, and Fustel de Coulanges. But while the contemporary usage can be traced directly to the influence of sociologists, the term has lost, at least in common parlance, much of the precision and nuance, as well as the historical perspective that it has in the sociological tradition. Because of this loss it has become something less than a sharp and precise tool for discussion.

In order to establish clearly the meaning "community" has in this book, let us rely on the definition of one of the outstanding students of the sociological tradition, the man who, perhaps more than any other, has contributed to the intellectual discussion of the quest for "community," Robert Nisbet.

> By community I mean something that goes far beyond mere local community. The word, as we find it in much nineteenth- and twentieth-century thought encompasses all forms of relationship which are characterized by a high degree of personal intimacy, emotional depth, moral commitment, social cohesion, and continuity in time. Community is founded on man conceived in his wholeness rather than in one or another of the roles, taken separately, that he may hold in a social order. It draws its psychological strength from levels of motivation deeper than those of mere volition or interest, and it achieves its fulfillment in a submergence of individual will that is not possible in unions of mere convenience or rational assent. Community is a fusion of feeling and thought, of tradition and commitment, of membership and volition. It

may be found in, or be given symbolic expression by, locality, religion, nation, race, occupation, or crusade. Its archetype, both historically and symbolically, is the family, and in almost every type of genuine community the nomenclature of family is prominent. Fundamental to the strength of the bond of community is the real or imagined antithesis formed in the same social setting by the non-communal relations of competition or conflict, utility or contractual assent. These, by their relative impersonality and anonymity, highlight the close personal ties of community.*

If we are to have a precise understanding of man's quest for community, we must see this quest in the analytical framework in which it was viewed by the great nineteenth century social analysts, for the connotations of their viewpoint still lurk around the word, usually left quite implicit, unfortunately.

These observers saw that the culture in which they were born and in which their ancestors had existed for many generations was slowly being eroded by the industrial revolution. The peasant village was being replaced by the industrial metropolis. The strong, stable, clearly understood relationships of post-feudal rural Europe were being replaced by the fluid, dynamic, contingent relationships of a new style of human existence which the world had previously not known. In the *community*—and the community par excellence was, of course, the farming village—a

* Robert Nisbet, *The Sociological Tradition* (New York: Basic Books, Inc., 1966), pp. 47-48.

man knew who he was and who he was not. He knew which actions were possible for him and which options were closed. He knew where he stood in his relatively stratified society.

But the very fact of stratification made it possible for relaxed and almost casual relationship across caste lines. If there were not many options open, neither was there much instability. The patterns of one's relationships were clear and foreordained; one knew what sort of social behavior was expected of him. Society was an organism; every man had a specific role to play, a role, however humble, honored by tradition. The most important relationships were rooted in blood, land, family, and tradition. Work and family, the Church and village reinforced one another, not, indeed, without some conflict and friction, but at least with the coherence that was possible when each of these institutions had the same limited horizons and the same traditional world view. There were many things that man did not have, but he did not lack roots.

The sociologist of the nineteenth century saw this post-feudal agricultural society being replaced by a rationalized, impersonal, formalized, and bureaucratized society in which man had few or no roots. In the new order, social relationships were apt to be highly limited and transitory, telling man very little as to who he was or what he ought to be doing. The ties of blood and land were replaced by the ties of legal contract; and the relationships with one's life-long friends and even one's life-long enemies were replaced by the cold, impersonal dealings one has with one's boss, one's neighbor in an apartment building, or one's bus driver. Sociologists like Weber and Tonnies were too realistic to think the change could be stopped, but neither could they hide their nostalgia for a past where, if there was less affluence, there was more humanity, and if there was more social control, there was also more social support.

Hardly anyone today would question the basic truth of the analysis. The transition from *gemeinschaft* (communal) to *gesellschaft* (industrial) society, to use Tonnies' terms, is one of the most dramatic changes in the style of living known to history. Social control over individual behavior has been weakened, and as a result there has been much greater freedom and material abundance; but warmth, intimacy, and social support have been lost, and society runs a serious risk of becoming slowly impersonal and dehumanized. It is not the purpose of this volume to discuss in detail what the prospects are for averting the highly mechanized existence which Tonnies and his colleagues thought they saw lying just over the horizon. Suffice it to say at the present time that, while they may have been inaccurate in some details, and may in the final analysis have been unduly pessimistic, the basic thrust of their analysis has proven quite accurate.

However, *gemeinschaft* has not died completely; in fact, a new tradition of sociological analysis has noted that it still is very much alive. The ethnic group, religion, and the informal face-to-face friendship group have kept alive the tradition of organic community in the face of the rationalizing tendencies of urbanism and industrialism. The face-to-face friendship group is still important in vastly different areas—for example, in determining levels of industrial production, in maintaining the morale of the military, in surveys of customer preferences, and in political campaigns. Man still seeks to associate with his "own kind" and to keep alive traditions and old ethnic values. One pastor in the west of Ireland was so plagued by American Irish coming to his parish house in search of the baptismal records of their ancestors that he had all the records of his parish put on microfilm. "The poor people," he said, "were just trying to find some roots for themselves, and I thought with microfilm we might make it a little bit easier for them."

The struggle, then, to keep alive some of the warmth, intimacy and support of the peasant village in the industrial society has not abated and probably will never abate. Tears shed for *gemeinschaft* may well have been premature. In our day, in addition, the quest for community has become quite conscious and explicit as modern man, particularly the youthful variety, has read, if not Weber and Tonnies, at least textbooks or popular sociology which adopt the sociological tradition for a frame of reference. "Community" has therefore become a useful category by which modern man attempts to have his cake and eat it, too; he would combine the affluence and material comforts of urban industrialism with the warmth and social support of the organic community of his ancestors.

Some comments must be made about this quest for community.

1. It is, first of all, a marvelous opportunity for the Church, which probably knows more about "community" and has had more experience with it than any other insti-

tution in the western world, and which, by its very nature as a meaning and belonging-providing institution is in a particularly strong strategic position, as we said in the first chapter, to respond to man's quest for community. For it would appear that implicit in the quest for community is a search for meaning which provides belonging, a belonging which, in turn, infuses one's life with meaning. Religion, of all the institutions of society, is the one best suited to provide permanent, profound, and intimate belonging precisely because it seeks to offer ultimate meaning, and the Catholic Church, which has always stressed this communitarian nature, is certainly a prime repository of both the theory and the practical resources to respond intelligently to the search for community.

2. Community is not, however, an unmixed blessing, and the somewhat nostalgic naiveté of the giants of the sociological tradition toward the *gemeinschaft* society that was being left behind ought not to be accepted without considerable reservations. While the community did tell a man who and what he was, it also told him, much oftener, what he was not and what he could not do. The post-feudal agricultural society of western Europe was not greatly removed from serfdom. There was, indeed, social support, but there were social constraints and controls which severely inhibited human freedom and dignity. A heavy price was paid to remain a member of the community; life was simplified largely because a man was forbidden so many options. The more creative and imaginative individuals in such communities must have found them incredibly oppressive, narrow, and stagnant. Scarcely any urban

American would be able to stand their narrowness, and rigidity for more than twenty-four hours. The community that was lost in the shift to urban industrialism would have made Sinclair Lewis's Gopher Prairie seem like Paris.

3. During most periods of history, in any contest between the individual and the community, the community won, at least in practice if not in theory. The individual existed for the community, which is to say that, generally, he existed for the benefit of the controlling powers in the community, and while he had some rights over against the community, the community had far more rights over against him. Breaking out of the bonds of the post-feudal agricultural community was one of the major steps forward on man's pilgrimage to freedom and self-fulfillment. Those who are so eager to restore community should beware of the dangers implicit in their project.

In the past, the intimate organic community meant social control and oppression for the individual, and this danger will not automatically be eliminated in any new forms of community now evolving. On the contrary, one has only to look at some of the aberrations of group dynamics presently masquerading as "Christian community" to see how strong the pressures for control really are, and how insidious are the temptations for manipulation and exploitation. The new communities which men are trying to build in their religious and civic life must be voluntary communities—communities based on free association, with the option to withdraw and the freedom to remain oneself guaranteed.

The danger of the community becoming restrictive and

narrow is all the more serious by reason of the availability of sophisticated social and psychological techniques which enable people to make other people *feel* that they are free, when in fact they are actually being controlled by others. The residual hunger of man to abandon his freedom, to lose himself in some sort of warm and all-protecting community is still strong, and if one wants to ponder the dangers in this escape from freedom, one need only recall the portentously powerful sense of community which the Nazis were able to generate in the sports plaza at Nüremberg.

In addition to being a threat to human freedom, a community can also cut people off from concerns which transcend its own limits. To those who lament the absence of community in the Church, we need only point to the ethnic parishes in many large cities. Such parish structures are a direct lineal descendent of the European *gemeinschaft*-type community, and they have notoriously failed to produce men and women with serious concerns beyond their own boundaries. We will discuss the Church's neighborhood community in greater detail in the next chapter, but it is sufficient to note at this point that communities are not always open-ended or outgoing, and that the history of communities has often enough been the history of people turning in upon themselves and ignoring the rest of the world.

4. Healthy human community grows slowly and organically, as people come to know and trust one another. It cannot be pushed; it cannot be created overnight. The pattern of multiple relationships which reinforce and

underlie each other develops only through time, and attempts to create instant community by psychological or sociological gimmickry are not only self-defeating and ludicrous, but they affront the dignity and the freedom of the human person. Given the long, unfortunate tradition of manipulation in the Catholic Church, new and more subtle forms of manipulation have an understandable appeal, especially when they can be justified in terms of the magic word "community," but manipulation they still are, and their pernicious influence must be resisted even when they masquerade in the guise of liberalism or of the New Left.

5. Nor can community be sought directly or self-consciously. Tonnies aptly called the self-conscious pursuit of community a *pseudo-gemeinschaft* phenomenon. Either our unities with our fellowmen grow out of common concerns, commitments, and common work, or they have no valid reality of their own. Community reflects existing commonalities and reinforces them, but it does not create them. Community is neither a goal nor a means. It is, rather, a side effect resulting from continued interaction between human beings. It enriches and facilitates more interaction but it must stem from and be rooted in this interaction. Men must have something to *do* together before they can become a community, and those who pursue community as an end in itself will be as disappointed as those who pursue happiness as an end in itself. Both community and happiness are "overspill" phenomena, not the result of direct striving.

6. Finally, voluntary community is difficult to achieve.

It requires sacrifice, adjustment, patience, generosity, and wisdom. It takes a long time, it endures many setbacks, and exacts a heavy price. Since it is based on friendship, the most noble of human sentiments, it can be, so long as it is voluntary, an extraordinarily rewarding human achievement. But as any man and woman who have tried to develop their marriage community will readily testify, community is not for the fainthearted dilettante, the superficial, or the weak.

In light of these assertions, it would follow that much of the talk about community in the contemporary Church is foolish and deceptive. Our goal must be to set about the work of the Church, and let community emerge from that work. We must convene, then, not to form communities; we must convene, rather, to be engaged in the work of the Kingdom—to announce the good news of the gospel, to bear witness to our joy and hope in the resurrection, and to serve the Lord in the least of our brothers. We do not have time to indulge in "creating community." We only have time to do the Lord's work, with the confidence that if we do this work together long enough, then we will become a community and will be grateful to the Lord for providing us with the opportunity for close friendship with our fellowmen.

We must also remove the obstacles that stand in the way of the emergence of communities from our common work. Community cannot exist as long as there are rigid and outmoded structures in the Church which separate men from their fellowmen and which insist more on rites, obligations, and duties, than on common membership in the

Church and common goals in the work of the Lord. Particularly obstructive are the caste distinctions which separate clergy from laity, and make the achievement of community, or even effective work, impossible. Further, community cannot come to be in the presence of authoritarian leadership which feels capable of making all of the decisions and insists, indeed, on making them, leaving no room for the intelligent participation of others in guiding and directing the emerging community. Finally, the grim sobriety which characterizes so much of the Church's effort, precludes the possibility of community. Since it is not easy, in any case, to form enduring friendships with our fellowmen, there must be joy and laughter in our emerging communities, for these are the climate required.

A priori theorizing about goals and means without any flexibility for the changes which experience dictates, creates an atmosphere in which meaningful community cannot survive for very long. And exploitation of other persons, whether explicit or implicit, deliberate or indeliberate, either aborts community or turns it into a constricting prison rather than a liberating friendship group. The most serious obstacle to community comes from the ancient human vices of distrust, fear, suspicion, and misunderstanding, vices by which we hide our selfhood from our fellowmen. He who is really interested in creating community in the Church ought not merely to proclaim the existence of community, or to invite people to join a community, or even attempt to compel them to join. Rather, he ought to devote his time and efforts to help his fellow Christians to eliminate distrust and fear from their lives and to improve the quality of their human relationships. For as the quality of these relationships improve, so does the possibility of a free and open community, in which men come together to reinforce each other, to sustain each other, to enrich each other, and to unite in prayers of gratitude to God for the blessing that is their community.

6 *The Church as Neighborhood*

The "neighborhood" grouping which characterizes many of our large cities is a crude and imperfect product of urban man's search for community. To some extent it meets man's need for primordial ties of land, blood, and fellowship. It is small enough to be comprehended, intimate enough to be supportive, and strong and stable enough to give some sense of durability and permanence. The neighborhood is probably a phenomenon of ethnic behavior, with roots in the ethnic ghettos of the past. One might hypothesize with some degree of confidence that those American cities which do not have strong neighborhood communities are precisely those which did not have heavy ethnic migration from 1880 to 1920. The relationship between the parish and the neighborhood can be best understood if the parish is viewed as an ethnic national Church which is both a cause and effect of the loyalty and cohesiveness of the neighborhood community.

The ethnic neighborhood with the parish church at its center was an extraordinarily useful asset to the Church when it was preoccupied with the question of "saving the faith" of the immigrant working class. Loyalty to the Church, loyalty to the parish, loyalty to the neighborhood, loyalty to one's ethnic group—all came virtually to the same thing, and one reason why the American Church did not lose the working class is the neighborhood ethnic parish, with its appeal to a complexus of human loyalties.

But there is more to the survival of the neighborhood, in American cities like Chicago or Detroit, than mere ethnic loyalty. Neighborhood parishes command almost as much devotion in the new suburbs as they did in the central city. The ethnic bond brought the inner-city neighborhood and neighborhood parish into being, but it is the quest for something relatively small and comprehensible in the seeming chaos of the metropolis which now *sustains* their existence. Unfortunately, as the work of the Church in the United States becomes more and more an ecumenical and metropolitan challenge, the neighborhood parish is not nearly the asset that it used to be; it can, on occasion, be a liability.

To state the problem in somewhat different terms, the conflict emerging is between the Church as a neighborhood institution and the Church as a neighborhood on pilgrimage. Pastoral work in the neighborhood must attempt to reconcile and relate these diverse dynamisms. The intimacy and social support, the loyalty and the comprehensibility which the neighborhood generates provide a favorable atmosphere in which the pastoral worker can train some of his flock to become citizens of the metropolis. Otherwise it tends to produce a narrowness, a defensiveness, and a rigidity which turns the Church into a local social service institution whose main task is to promote the stability of the neighborhood. The tension between these two poles will never be finally resolved in any parish, because the majority of the parishioners will remain steadfastly "local". But a few will exhibit metropolitan tendencies. The task of the pastoral worker, one supposes, is to increase, as much as he can, the number of these metropolitans.

There is an ancient debate in Catholic lay circles about the role of the parish in neighborhood problems, one group holding that it belongs to the laity simply as citizens, the other holding, much more realistically it seems to me, that since the parish is a neighborhood institution and its pastor is a neighborhood leader, both pastor and parishioners *as such* must be involved in neighborhood problems. Curiously enough, many of the members of the first group, who would wish to exclude pastors in white or integrating neighborhoods from community organizations, do not hesitate to cheer when priests in *Negro* neighborhoods march in picket lines!

The problem of the involvement of the Church and the clergy in *specific* problems is not soluble on the theoretical level. Virtually everyone will agree, if pushed, that there are some problems which the Church cannot escape being involved in, and other problems which the Church would be well-advised to avoid. The difficulty, of course, is how to classify a specific problem. The author would caution, in any event, that while in theory there are some issues in which the clergy most assuredly should take the initiative, nonetheless, priests should exercise restraint and careful thought about joining in active politics on the community level, whether it be the politics of the picket line or of the community organization. To say that priests should exercise restraint is not to say that they should stay out of the problems; it is merely to say that they should be convinced before they undertake political activity, that it is, indeed, essential for them to be involved in the particular issue at hand.

But the debate about the involvement of the Church in neighborhood politics seems to miss the main point. The issue is not whether the Church should be involved in the neighborhood, but rather what kind of neighborhood involvement is going to provide an opportunity for at least some of the members of the neighborhood to expand their horizons to the metropolis. The issue is whether to have an open parish or a closed parish—a parish working for an open neighborhood or a parish striving to keep the neighborhood closed.

The very terms "open" and "closed," of course, bring to mind the issue of racial integration. But as long as the problems of metropolitan living are seen as essentially problems of racial integration, the integration problem itself, perhaps the most serious problem the metropolis faces, will never be solved. Even if there were no racial problems in America, the closed neighborhood would still be a liability to metropolitan living, and the Church would still have a mission to strive for the opening of the neighborhood, or at least the opening of some eyes of the neighborhood, to the vision of the *metropolitan* community, quite beyond the narrow neighborhood.

It must be confessed that few urban parishes have been

successful at this task, or have even tried very hard. The organizational thrust of a local parish is toward its own problems and the problems of the neighborhood in which it is immersed. It must build a school, pay its debts, keep the parking lot free of snow in the winter time, educate its children, marry its young people, and bury its dead. It is very difficult for it not to become jealous of its own independence, and yet more difficult for it to learn how to cooperate even with neighboring Catholic parishes, with other religious groups, and with city-wide staffs and organizations. The typical Catholic parish seems to become aware of the community beyond itself only when it is threatened by invasion from another ethnic group, and such a threat usually moves the parish to action only long after it is too late to do anything constructive about the problem. Hardly one has yet dealt successfully with the "changing neighborhood" situation.

The process is depressingly the same: one parish is dying and another is being born, and for a time the two parishes and neighborhoods coexist in a state of mutual hostility, suspicion, and occasional open conflict. The dying parish is paying the price for its parochialism in the past, and for the parochialism of hundreds of neighborhoods in the metropolis which refuse to concede that a metropolitan problem is their problem until it threatens their security.

It is perhaps unrealistic to blame a parish for being parochial, but one can certainly blame a pastoral worker for being parochial, for he is precisely the one who ought to be the seer and the prophet of the neighborhood community; the one who stirs up a vision of the world beyond the neighborhood; who leads the Church as a neighborhood institution only after he has grasped and taken charge of the Church as a neighborhood on pilgrimage. The pastor as leader of a pilgrimage must concern himself *primarily* not with building the school, shoveling the snow, paying the debt, or repairing the boiler, but with those parishioners who show any real potential for emerging as citizens of the metropolis. For finally, it is only the metropolitans who can fashion a city in which the neighborhood itself will be able to survive.

Thus, in the many parishes where "New Communities" are beginning to emerge, the pastor, far from viewing them with suspicion or distrust, should look to them as a source of the leadership the parish will need if it is to begin its "pilgrimage." The pastoral worker may choose to ignore these groups, when the masses of his parish are faithful church-goers who often receive the sacraments, contribute to and support the parish efforts, and enroll their children in the parish school. If the Negro ghetto is not moving in his direction, he may even do this for a long time without serious "trouble" in his parish. But let him make no mistake about it, the parish which is not metropolitan, which is not ecumenical, not on a pilgrimage beyond the boundaries of the neighborhood, is in our day not worthy of being called either Christian or Catholic, and neither (we are compelled to say) is the pastor who leads it.

It is extremely difficult, in discussing the neighborhood and its parish, to avoid extremes. The glorification of the neighborhood parish which has become almost dogma in the American Church is an error, but it would be equally erroneous to reject the values which the local parish embodies. It is a mistake to be so local that one has no metropolitan view, but equally it would be a mistake to think that broad interests can be long-sustained by most human beings unless they have local roots. The social forces which have produced the neighborhood and the neighborhood parish cannot be ignored or resisted. Man cherishes the parcel of land where he lives and loves, where he raises his children and makes his friends, where he can retreat a little from the confusion of the world of work. The neighborhood represents, in much less developed fashion, the same community-building instinct of modern man which has produced the "New Community." The pastoral worker who ignores such instincts or tries to destroy them is making as great a mistake as the pastoral worker who yields to them completely. Gilbert Chesterton, in *Napoleon of Notting Hill,* has underlined the paradox that man is simultaneously local and metropolitan in the big city, and that he cannot really be one unless he is also the other.

It is not an easy task that confronts the pastoral worker. Most of his parishioners will be resolutely local, and no power on earth or in heaven, or even under the earth will greatly alter their myopia. The few metropolitans may well be alienated from the local neighborhood, and while they may be effective workers on the level of the metropolis, they surely will not be able to lead their neighbors, nor, perhaps, even solve the problems of the metropolis, because they do not understand the values of the neighborhood.

But not so very many people are needed, after all. It is not necessary for a majority of the parishioners or even for a very substantial minority to be simultaneously local and metropolitan. Only a handful—a dozen or so, to choose a number not exactly at random—might do. But if a pastor can find such apostles, these represent the hope of the parish and the hope of the city. Everything and everyone else in the parish should take second place.

7 The Church as "New Community"

A good deal of publicity has been given lately to the emergence of "the Underground Church," or "the hidden Church," or "the silent schism."* The names have been used to cover a wide variety of phenomena—selectivity in doctrinal beliefs and moral practices, experimental and avant garde liturgy generally celebrated in private homes, the emergence of new and independent lay organizations, and even the curious phenomenon of Pentecostal Catholicism. These rather diverse phenomena tell us something important about the contemporary Church. The revolution begun by Vatican Council II shook the confidence of many Catholics in existing ecclesiastical institutions, and a wide variety of new institutions began to appear almost spontaneously. Some of them are very much a part of the organized Church and some so far removed that their claim to be Catholic is perhaps dubious. Most of them represent various degrees of impatience with the ambigu-

* For a responsible treatment of this development, see *The Underground Church*, edited by Malcolm Boyd (New York: Sheed & Ward, 1968).

ous response of the organized Church to the forces released at the Council.

It would be a mistake, however, to lump all of these innovations under one heading. Many of the Pentecostal groups are an obvious form of delusional hysteria, though perhaps a relatively harmless form. And some liturgical innovation demonstrates a lack both of good theology and good taste, while some of the independent lay groups are more interested in fighting clergy than in anything else. But it is probably safe to say that these few are obvious aberrations, and that the fundamental event for the Catholic Church in the post-Vatican era is the emergence of what we have called the "New Community," the small, fellowship groups of Catholics bound together, usually around the liturgy, to deepen their religious life and to support each other's work in the world beyond the Church. *To focus on the aberrations and peculiarities is to overlook the striking lesson that such groups have to teach the Church.*

The "New Community" means, if it means anything, that a minority, but an extremely important and dedicated minority of Catholics, no longer finds its religious needs satisfied in the traditional large urban parish. Small informal fellowship bands of believers are but the surface of the iceberg of the personalist and communitarian revolution within the Church and within the whole of Western society. The largest corporate bureaucracies, political, economic, military, and ecclesiastical, grow bigger and more complex, as the sophisticated technology of modern life demands ever larger expenditures of money, more complex technology, and more long-range planning. In many if not most instances, these large corporate structures show little or no concern for the community-forming instinct of their members. But whether the technical structure or the ecclesiastical structure likes it or not, modern man is bent on having community, and the self-conscious personalism of the new ecclesiastical community merely represents in the Church the manifestation of modern man's conscious search for authentic, honest, and trusting human relationships. The powerful assertion of this development is not going to be changed. The denizen of the techno-structure will not be satisfied with religion that is not based on intimacy and fellowship. Not all of them will seek for a religious group to meet these needs, but if religion does not at least attempt to respond to the demands for intimacy and fellowship, it will not have very much effect in the modern world. To repeat, this is not to say that religion is in the community-forming business; men will form their own communities whether religion chooses to approve or not. The point is, rather, that only the most naive pastoral worker will attempt to ignore the community-forming instinct, and even if one attempts to do so, he will find rising up, to face and condemn him the irrepressible "New Community."

Just as the local neighborhood in its community-providing dimension can easily have negative effects on human society, so the smaller new religious groups, the "New Community," is not necessarily good in itself. The small fellowship of Christians may be Gnostic and narcissistic. It can disguise subtle forms of aggression under the pretext of honesty. It can turn from a religious into a psychoanalytic group, more interested in prayerful therapy than in prayer. It can mobilize group pressures and deprive its members of freedom. It can be so concerned with its own narrow interests that it ignores the rest of the Church and the rest of the world. It can be so involved with its own problems and its own joys that it will, for all practical purposes, secede from the human race. It can turn into a social club where fun and games replace the hard work of the apostolate.

But, we repeat, this "New Community" cannot be stopped. It is the religious manifestation of the quest of contemporary man for meaning and belonging. The institutional Church may oppose it, but it will do so at a terrible price, and will not be successful. It may ignore it, as it seems to be doing now, and miss a magnificent opportunity, or it may watch the "New Community" closely and learn from it and use this learning in much of its work. It is not an exaggeration to say that a sophisticated understanding of the forces that have brought the "New Community" into being may well be the most effective knowledge that the pastoral worker can have.

Not everyone wishes to join a new community. The intense intimacy and fellowship of such small religious groups would be too much for some people and would simply not be of interest to those who have decided that religion is not an important part of their life. Not everyone clearly understands his own needs. But a broader pastoral program which takes into account the dynamics of the "New Community" will be far more effective than one which does not. The recognition and utilization of man's quest for meaningful belonging ought to be a *leitmotif* running through all contemporary pastoral work.

Obviously such a pastoral approach will require a major redistribution of pastoral efforts because, as one looks at the new communities which are emerging around the country, one can see much in them that is completely absent from normal pastoral work in the Catholic Church and in other churches, too. Parishes tend to be formal and well-organized; the "New Community" is informal and casual. Parishes tend to be monarchical, or at least aristocratic; the new communities are authentically collegial, with consensus required on almost all decisions. There is a certain stiffness and reserve about most parochial congregations; the new communities tend to be emotionally extroverted. The parish is tied down with property and fixed obligations; the "New Community" is free-wheeling and mobile. While the parish has clear and definite notions about what it can and cannot do, the "New Community" is "open-ended" and tends to ask not *why*, but *why not*? The parish is large, the "New Community" is small, not exceeding the number beyond which common friendship is impossible. The parish views itself as the Church in miniature, the "New Community" views itself rather as a sect which hardly can reflect all of the elements of the Church. The parish views the Church as an orderly collection of congregations like itself, whereas the "New Community" must view the Church as an aggregation of sects which proliferate at will, and which can be dramatically different, one from another.

When the "New Community" is described in this fashion, it represents a rather disturbing phenomenon. It is a very different religious manifestation than that which most Catholics have known all their lives and for which most pastoral workers were trained, though it bears a close resemblance to Christianity in its origins and to many of the most dynamic and creative groups that have emerged through the history of the Church.

The typical Catholic parish, or Protestant congregation, for that matter, is not a new community and can never be one. Many, if not most, parishioners would not want to belong to the "New Community" groups, but the parish must be broad enough to tolerate and encourage the existence of new communities within its boundaries, and it must regard the people who are members of such communities as leaders in revitalizing the rest of the parish according to the values which animate the "New Community." For if these values cannot be found to some degree in a Christian parish, that parish will really be able to engage in a merely formal, external Christianity, which has little to do with the spread of the Gospel and is completely out of touch with the social, psychological, and philosophical currents of the times.

Many people who must deal with members of the new communities find their enthusiasm is somewhat difficult to tolerate, and their assumption that they have found *the* answer, quite unpleasant. But neither of these reactions is particularly relevant. If one is to understand the power and the wisdom of the "New Community," one must look at it in its finer manifestations. One must witness their joy, and the courageous outlook which profound Christian charity, exercised in a small group of people, can generate. And when one has witnessed this, he finds it somewhat easier to be persuaded that the New Community could be, if not *the* answer, at least one very important answer; that indeed it might reveal to us the key to pastoral work in contemporary America.

The most serious problem in the New Community, however, is not that it is underground, for presumably the need for that will shortly come to an end. Nor is the problem that on occasion its liturgical practices are both illicit and doctrinally and historically unsound, and wanting in good taste, for the passage of time will cure that. The most serious problem the New Community encounters springs up from the human condition, and always plagues man's interaction with his fellowmen: because of its small size and the intensity of relationships among its members, the New Community quickly exposes in its members the basic obstacles to Christian friendship and love. More like a family than an organization, it reveals people to others as plainly as they are known in the family environment. It drops many masks—"friendliness," urbanity, charm—which we maintain for the world outside the family. The distractions of size and complexity of larger organizations are missing; instead, the fears, suspicions, distrust, rivalries, envies, competitiveness, animosities, ambivalences, dislikes, and hatreds which man keeps hidden in ordinary social life, surface rapidly and unequivocally. In this respect, the model of the New Community is perhaps the twelve Apostles, striving for preference, easily slighted, often contentious. The repressions that hold back our selfishness, our distrust, and our rivalry are eliminated in small intimate circles, and we discover how easily sharp conflicts arise. This problem deserves some analysis.

The New Community is rather like a romance. There is, first of all, a tremendous burst of excitement and joy as we discover someone who thinks as we do, shares our values, and apparently is willing to accept us and love us as persons. Then there is wariness, as the other gets too close to us and begins to make demands upon us, begins to know our weaknesses as well as our strengths. He (or she) is getting too close, invading the psychic boundaries which we have drawn around our inner self, beginning to know us as we really are, and that's a risk few of us are willing to take.

The only saving reaction to this second phase is trust; that is to say, we must be confident enough of our friends and ourselves to put away the second level of masks that we wear. In interaction beyond the family, we pretend to be polite and charming; in the family situation we often pretend to be ugly, mean, and suspicious, when in fact, we are only fearful. And if we can put away the defense mechanisms of meanness and suspicion that fear generates, we can really be ourselves—a self which is generally far superior to the superficially pleasant self we present in life beyond the limits of the family. But few of us are strong enough in our selfhood to be able to trust others with ease, and we would much prefer, if we had our choice, to live in a state of armed coexistence, or of real affability, just short of trusting intimacy, as long as we possibly can, because if

we do open ourselves to others in trust and permit them to
know us as we really are, we fear that they will see us as
empty and worthless, and maybe run roughshod over us.

When a religious community finds itself in the midst of
this second phase, getting very close to trust and yet holding back, it is in for weary, painful, and difficult months. It
may collapse, it may turn into a therapy group, it may take
out its aggressions in intense social action, or in an esoteric
flight which isolates it from the realities of human life.
The therapeutic temptation is the most serious because,
while a new community struggling toward trust does need
some therapy to facilitate communication and friendship
among its members, it is not designed, presumably, to become a therapeutic group. There is an important distinction between group therapy and therapy for a group. The
New Community will have a therapeutic side-effect, but
given its nature as a religious community, this must never
be its goal.

Eventually, the break-through will come, perhaps
slowly, or even on occasion, all at once, and people will
begin to trust each other. Authentic human friendship will
begin to flourish, though there will be many trials and
pains, many regressions and new beginnings, as in any relationship among friends. How many of the New Communities will survive this trial is problematic, especially since
it is not clear that very many people who become involved
in such projects are fully aware of what they are undertak-
ing. Many groups will collapse, others will become esoteric, still others, as we have said, will become perpetual
self-therapies, but a few will become profoundly Christian

leavens. One does not need very many of these to substantially change the Church and the world.

Naively enthusiastic conveners of community—those cultists who find their community invigorating and reassuring in facing the problems of life—are not likely to have the courage, faith, and patience it takes when the elements assail the New Community. If they were more realistic in their expectations in the beginning, their disappointments and frustrations, as time goes on, would not so greatly endanger the cohesion of their group.

But given the vigor with which the underground is spreading and the naiveté with which many are flocking to it, one can expect great difficulty, conflict, and distress, as simultaneously in many parts of the country many different New Communities encounter envy and suspicion. There are a few very unpleasant years ahead of them, if they are not going to drop out of the best and hardest of schools—the school of love.

8 The Church as Worship

One of the great disappointments in contemporary Catholicism is the failure of the liturgical revival to develop real social consciousness in Catholics. The failure has been pointed out clearly enough by Daniel Callahan:

> The first thing which makes me doubt this faith (in the Liturgy) is the accumulating testimony of many active liturgists based on practical experience. A liturgical reform by itself does not in fact guarantee that congregations will turn their gaze outward to the world. All the early hopes on this point will come to grief. I see no reason to expect that some kind of liturgical miracle will take place which will give lie to this accumulating pastoral experience . . . Despite all the engaging theory, no pedagogical task has proved so difficult as that of getting the great masses of Catholics to see the connection between the Liturgy and world . . .*

* "Putting the Liturgy In Its Place," *National Catholic Reporter,* August 9, 1967.

It should have been perfectly clear that a renewed Liturgy, while it would be very important to the life of Christians, could hardly be expected by itself to produce even a limited number of dedicated and enthusiastic Christians. But the liturgical enthusiasts did not claim that it was going to produce a limited number; they claimed that the renewed Liturgy would transform the entire membership of the Church. It was a naive claim. From the point of view of social science, a sensible and realistic claim for a wholly renewed Liturgy would be that it is indispensable as *part* of the religious formation of *most* members of the Christian *elite*. Mankind knows few effective elite groups which do not have their own ritual. Ritual is important not merely as a symbol of the unity and commitment which holds the elite together, but also as a strong psychological reinforcement of their unity and commitment. To understand how this can be, we must say something about the role of prayer, and particularly communal prayer in man's life.

There are a number of observations which social science enables us to make about prayer, perhaps the most important of which is that even if there were not a God, man would still have to pray. The prayer phenomenon is universal in human cultures and peoples, and while it can run all the way from magic to mystical contemplation, it seems in almost every instance to be the manifestation of the human need to express dependency. We are conscious that we depend upon the beneficent forces in the universe and upon our fellowmen for survival—that we cannot "go it alone." The primitive, attempting to barter with the good and evil spirits through his magical rites, and the saint lost in the third degree of infused contemplation, both acknowledge that there are forces and powers in the universe beyond their control.

The modern exposé of "secular theology" would have us believe that contemporary man, because of his scientific advancement, no longer feels the need for "myths" or for prayer. Such an assertion is demonstrably false. Scientific progress, no matter how impressive, does not ultimately take the "chanciness" out of human life, nor does it give man anything like complete control of the world in which he lives. Contemporary man may well be less dependent than were his predecessors, but dependent he still is, and it really does him very little good to pretend that he is not. If statistical data are to be believed, most men are by no means persuaded of their independence, even in our scientific age, and at least in times of trouble and difficulty, they return to prayer.

But there is more in prayer than the mere acknowledgement of dependence. Prayer is also, and perhaps in the final analysis more importantly, an attempt at union. The native bargaining with the spirits wants, if only in an economic fashion, to unite himself with the good spirits; and the mystic wishes to lose himself in the contemplation of goodness. Man sees good and evil about him in the world and has a powerful urge to ally himself with the good, partly because it seems prudent to do so and partly because his personality drives him to seek that which is good. Prayer, then, is not only a quest for security, but also a search for union with goodness.

Finally, in almost all societies, men pray *together,* as

though there were universal acceptance of the fact that the quest for security and for goodness must be a joint quest, even though mystics may depart from the community at least in some societies, for their mystical experience. In many, if not in most societies, ecstasy occurs not as an isolated act but as part of the community worship. It is as though man suspects that he can find the sources of power and goodness which dominate the universe, at work in some fashion in his relationships with his fellowmen. God is present not only "out there," but also "here among us," and the human race really did not need Bishop Robinson to confirm this insight.

We pray, therefore, whether we be priest or layman, because we have to pray; because prayer is the acknowledgement of the long human experience that without it we are something less than human. Prayer is not an option. It flows from man's need to unite himself with his fellowmen in union with the forces of good and with the power on which he feels dependent, and which at least in many instances, he desires to serve. Such public prayer activities frequently produce an ecstasy, which is to say that man goes out of himself, stands "beside himself," and senses in an extraordinarily powerful way his unity with the higher Power, with the forces of nature, with his fellowmen, and even with himself. But we need not look merely at the extreme of ecstasy, which puts the worshiper in some form of trance. The study of collective behavior shows that many different communal activities produce something of an ecstatic effect on the human personality—crowds at football games, political rallies, mob actions—all demonstrate the power of collective behavior to tap pent-up potentials of human interpersonal behavior.

Liturgy thus can play a powerful role in the life of man. For most men it is important only at the critical junctures of life—birth, sickness, danger, marriage, death—and for those men whose religious inclinations do not rise above the average, almost any sort of liturgical form will do. It need not be intelligible; it need not even move them very much out of their ordinary patterns of behavior; it need only reassure them that they have paid the due and proper reverence to the forces presiding over the universe.

To this somewhat passive majority, the change in liturgical form may not be objectionable but neither is it very exciting. They may rejoice at a vernacular liturgy and may even get some emotional kicks out of hymn singing, but there is no reason in the world to expect a transformation in their lives because of any liturgical change, no matter how dramatic or "relevant" it may be.

But among religious elites, and particularly those whose socio-psychological style involves what we have previously called a "non-instrumental" approach to religion, a new liturgical format may be not only very important, but absolutely essential.

However, it is also important to understand what kind of liturgy is most likely to respond to the needs and expectations of such a religious elite. It is very unlikely, except on a rare occasion, that a liturgical experience, no matter how moving, will actually create an empirical community. All the evidence from the social sciences suggests the contrary, that the liturgical experience is a manifestation and a very powerful reenforcement of a *pre-existing* human community. The thought that liturgy can create community where none exists is, from the viewpoint of social science, extraordinarily unrealistic. For community is a shared experience of those who already share other experiences, and it manifests both the sharing and the experience. It is a communion of those already in union. It will inspire people to practice the charity symbolized in liturgical service, only if a measure of union and charity already exist among the members of the liturgical group before they come together in worship.

Here, precisely, is the error in suggesting that charity and service ought to take first place over liturgy. The two are correlatives and not contradictories. Liturgy reenforces service, but shared service makes liturgy possible. He who does not serve others in charity, who is not united at least with his follow worshipers in the close, generous, and unselfish relationships of charity, has really nothing to celebrate in the liturgical experience. But on the other hand, he who does not summon the powerful latent forces of collective behavior to the practice of his charity through collective worship runs a serious risk of seeing his charity turn sterile, rigid, and unproductive.

One may urge that there are many secularists who seem able to practice charity without liturgy. We could quibble and say that, in many instances, the secularist charity is singularly unloving, or that the secularists are not without their own liturgical format, but the quibble would be irrelevant. Granted that there are *some* men who can practice charity without liturgy, it does not follow that *most*

men can do so, even most members of religious elites, nor
does it follow that their charity would not be stronger or
more human if it were integrated into a meaningful experience of collective worship.

It is, therefore, obvious what true liturgical renewal requires if it is to be pastorally productive. Quite apart from
new formats of worship, or Offertory processions or English Canons, folk masses, guitar music, sermons on the
Liturgy, or vestments of raw silk (or no vestments), fussi-
ness, neo-rubricism, or tasteless innovations, liturgical renewal must be geared to man's community-making propensities and, in fact, be a celebration of bonds of affection
and love which *already* unite man with his fellowmen. It
must renew, strengthen, and extend to the world the charity which *already exists* among people who are deeply concerned for one another. All liturgical reforms and experi-
mentations, if they are to be pastorally effective, must be
geared to such a goal. Liturgy must be a meaningful experience of union already in some fashion perceived, or it is
no experience at all. It lacks supporting bonds.

This is not to say that English Canons (now available in
four variations) or folk music or Offertory processions are
objectionable. They may be very useful, but only in the
context of a broader goal of celebrating union and love.

The Roman Liturgy in its present half-renewed state *is* a
rather poor instrument for such celebration, though anyone who has experienced a meaningful liturgy, one which
does reflect the love in the group, particularly the small
group, can report that even in its present format the
Roman Liturgy is capable of providing meaningful religious experience. Also, if the rumors from the Under-

ground Church are correct, some of the tasteful and theologically accurate experimental liturgies are extraordinarily moving.

In the Underground Church there are, of course, some absurdities. And many emotions released at its worship have nothing to do with charity or service. Liturgy, like the community which it celebrates, can be either dysfunctional or functional for the growth of the human spirit. But the point is not that Liturgy can be abused, nor even that Liturgy may release dangerous emotions. The point is, rather, that religiously committed people need Liturgy, and that at the present time, in the American Church, the choice is not between experimental Liturgy and non-experimental Liturgy (at least, for the elite), but rather between good experiments and bad experiments—between experiments that understand the powerful forces liturgical worship can release, and experiments which merely play with the emotions that are tapped by collective behavior. To repeat, we are no longer faced with the possibility, at least for religious elites, of a non-demonic Liturgy; the question is whether it will release good spirits or bad spirits.

Effective Liturgy will work only with small pre-existing communities, and the official parochial Liturgy should strive to imitate the style of such fellowship groups. It must both move and be moving; must not be so obscure as to exclude human emotions, nor so slow and poky as to dull them. It must use vital symbols, those which have real meaning, which engage the mind, heart, and soul of all present.

Further, the Liturgy must be flexible and open to experimentation. A rigid and "frozen" Liturgy is not alive, and a Liturgy that is not alive, while it may serve to mark rites of passage, is of no use to the elite.

Finally, an authentic Liturgy in the contemporary world must be sacred, despite the efforts of the secularist to demythologize it. As we have pointed out earlier, Liturgy deals precisely with that area which demythologizers attempt to rule out of human existence—the non-rational, the primordial, the demonic, and the sacred. The secularists would have us believe that for modern scientific man these tendencies have been eliminated. Everett C. Hughes, one of the great sociologists of the twentieth century, has stated our own view quite movingly:

> Those who have the cure of souls—pastors and psychiatrists—can tell better than I what burdens break and what sicknesses ravage the souls of those, who, in the name of self-reliance, emancipation or progress, try to act as if there were no cycle of youth, maturity, old age and death; no rhythms of inner peace and conflict, of guilt and freedom from guilt, of grief and of the healing of its wound . . .
>
> How ghastly can be the smile of a suffering man who is pretending that all is well; how pathetic the stiff but tottering stance of a man who, because he does not know how to share his troubles with others through the historic liturgies, is about to break under them. How pathetic, also, the man who, in his time of trouble, expresses the ultimate of that individualism in which we have all been reared, the insistence that

his troubles are so private and so unique that no social salve can soothe them.*

Liturgy, therefore, must be sacred. It must not only be
an experience of man's communion with his fellowmen,
but also of their communion precisely in those primordial
forces that are most obvious in ordinary communion with
his fellows but which transcend that daily experience. Liturgy must be, for the modern post-Vatican II Christian,
what it has always been for anyone who has engaged in
liturgical worship through the whole course of man's history—an experience of God present among us.

---

* Everett C. Hughes, *Men and Their Work* (Chicago: University of
Chicago Press, 1959) pp. 17-18.

9 The Church as Diocese

In the strictly theological sense, the bishop is the parish priest of the diocese, and the diocese is a "church" which, in union with the other dioceses, form "the Church." Surely this was the way St. Paul thought of the organizational structure of the church, and it seems to be very much the way the Fathers of Vatican Council II thought of it, also. Once again, however, theology presents the goal and the ideal, and Church history the practical reality. The bishop was at one time the "president" of the Christian community in a city, and the handful of priests were his staff.

But the diocese is no longer the single parish in a city; it has evolved from a single parish to the bureaucracy we know today. It is difficult to see how, in the modern world, such an evolution could have been prevented, although it may well be that diocesan bureaucracies have taken on many functions which are not at all inherent in the nature of a diocese, and which, being both many and complex, prevent efficient administration. The modern diocese stands, historically, somewhere between the *gemeinschaft* community of the ancient parish and an efficient modern corporation; it is too bureaucratic to provide religious community, and yet not bureaucratic enough (that is to say, not efficient enough bureaucratically) to create an atmosphere in which lesser groups can develop and flourish within it. The diocese is too centralized to have the personal touch, yet not centralized enough to be effective.

There are two basic weaknesses in the governance of many, if not most American dioceses which make for this combination of impersonality and inefficiency. The first is the mistake of *amateurism*. American Catholicism seems to be obsessed with the conviction that anybody can do anything, which is translated at the level of diocesan administration to mean that Canon lawyers can do everything. Whatever is to be said of Canon Law, and truly some of the brightest and most creative American clergy are the younger members of the Canon Law Association of America, it does not seem that a degree in Canon Law equips one to be a personnel administrator or financial officer, planner and coordinator, a public relations expert, and a prophet. Nonetheless, these are the roles which chancery officials, most of them trained in Canon Law, are forced to play in the American Church. It is not surprising that the roles are not always played well, though it is somewhat surprising that they are played as well as they are as frequently as they are.

The second fallacy is that of monarchism, which presumes that, not only can Canon lawyers do everything, but that ultimately one man, whether his training be in Canon

Law or not, must do everything. Many American dioceses are greatly over-centralized because their bishops reserve all major and many minor decisions to themselves. There may be some psychological explanation for this, if one wishes to search out detailed information on the personalities of those selected to be bishops, but one need not go this far. The social structural explanations are quite sufficient. Given the way the American diocese is ordered, and indeed, the way Canon Law presumes the bishop operates, it is almost necessary for a bishop to be an expert on all things.

This style of diocesan administration, enshrined in Canon Law and traditional procedure, dates from an era when the Church was much less involved in organizational complexities. The results of thus putting new wine into old skins can be extremely unfortunate. If the bishop tries to keep up with an amount of detailed administrative responsibility which he cannot hope to handle effectively, he becomes more and more an administrator and less and less a leader and a pastor. His time is consumed with getting things done, and he has relatively little time for the charismatic role of influencing the minds and hearts of men, a role which, as John Kenneth Galbraith has observed in another context, is not only the most important, but may be the only one left for the top leader in the structure of society.

This conversion of the bishop into an administrator has become so accepted that it is often thought to be a high compliment to say of a candidate for the episcopal office that he is "a good administrator," when administration is precisely the sort of thing which ideally the bishop, as teacher and leader, should be spared. Furthermore, the expenditure of episcopal time for administrative chores is not only religiously dysfunctional; it is administratively inefficient, precisely because most of the administrative work of the bishops concerns details which, in secular organizations of comparable size, the president would not dream of touching.

Several reforms are therefore necessary in the diocesan administration. Competent technicians must be added to chancery staffs to supervise the financial, personnel, planning, educational, organizational, and public relations functions of the diocese. Whether these technicians are priests or lay people matters much less, in my judgment, than whether they are well trained, and have adequate security and high professional standards in their roles.

Provided with such a staff, the men who are chosen to be bishops should be scholars, dreamers, and prophetic visionaries who can interpret the meaning of the Gospel for their diocese in light of the problems of the modern world. The combination of a higher degree of professionalization in the second level of diocesan administrations, and greater emphasis on charisma in the first level ought to produce dioceses in which efficiency and vision can be combined, as they are in many other large American corporate structures.

In the large urban dioceses and archdioceses, a considerable amount of reorganization will also have to take place in which some functions carried on at the local level, such as purchasing, architectural designing, financial supervision, and educational administration, will be centralized. Other functions, particularly pastoral ones, such as youth work, vocation recruiting, family education, and work with community organizations, will be decentralized so that smaller groups, closer to neighborhood problems, can exercise a maximum amount of initiative and responsibility. Professionalization, some decentralization combined with selective centralization, and emphasis on the pastoral role of the leader of the diocese will no more restore the single-parish diocese of the past than a modern metropolis will revert to a collection of peasant villages. But such administrative reorganization, which is certainly in keeping with modern corporate practice and could be accomplished rather easily, must be considered the first step in the revitalization of dioceses and their organizational structures, a revitalization which must come relatively quickly, if the American diocese, as we now know it, is to survive for very long.

Other reforms will be necessary, too, however, before the diocese acquires the kind of vitality that is necessary to make it an effectively functioning unit in the Church universal. Chief among these reforms is—and it is not too strong a word—the democratization of the diocese. Nothing more is being urged here than that which existed in the early Church: participatory roles for the clergy and the laity in selecting its leadership, and in determining the broad outlines of diocesan policy whereby the work of preaching the Gospel is to be implemented within the diocesan Church. The documents of the recent Vatican Council already call for the establishment of consultative councils of the clergy and laity, although such institutions have been relatively slow in coming into existence in the United States, and it is not yet clear how much power they will have or how representative they will be. One is forced to observe, from the viewpoint of political sociology, that if such institutions are not representative and do not have considerable power, they simply will not be taken seriously and will, indeed, be a waste of time. The emergence of the unofficial clergy and lay associations around the country are clear indications that clergy and laity alike have considerable reservations about the viability of the official consultative bodies (even though there is room for both the official and unofficial organizations).

It takes heroic trust on the part of the bishop to establish consultative organizations which will be anything more than rubber stamps for episcopal decision-making. In fact (as some bishops are aware), it does not make much difference whether one calls such organizations merely consultative or not, because one ignores the advice of such weighty consultative bodies only rarely and at the risk of considerable difficulty. It is indeed dangerous to entrust such power to one's clergy and laity, but if one does not do so, collegiality is meaningless, and the alternative is an authoritarianism which is outmoded, inefficient, and in practice, unchristian.

Furthermore, it is much wiser to deal openly and fearlessly with an official organization than to run the risk of seeing an unpredictable and undependable unofficial organization assume responsibilities on its own initiative. To put the matter more bluntly, if the College of Priests and the Assembly of Laity are not given power, the informal associations will *take* power. Such a democratization of the Church may seem monstrously inefficient, but as Winston Churchill remarked, democracy is a terribly inefficient way of running a society until one looks at the alternatives.

It is also quite clear that in the future, and hopefully in the not too distant future, bishops will be elected by their priests and people. It is time the American Church returned to the wisdom of its first bishop, John Carroll, who said that in a society like the United States, this is the only appropriate way to select a bishop. One could add that in most of the countries of the modern world also, it is the only appropriate way to select a bishop, not to mention that it is the older, traditional way, too long neglected. Such a change will undoubtedly be strongly resisted because it could very well mean the end of the power structures that presently exist, and no one willingly gives up one's power or that of his class. It is to be hoped that those responsible for such change will realize how much harm the present anachronistic method of selecting bishops actually does to the Church, precisely because it offers little guarantee that the bishop will be responsive to the needs, problems, and aspirations of his people. A leader who cannot so respond is a leader foredoomed to failure.

In the reorganization of the diocese, serious consideration will have to be given to the role of various diocesan organizations. Many of the existing ones, the Councils of Catholic Men and Women, for example, while they may make some pretense at representing the rank and file membership, are little more than fronts for diocesan officials who choose the leaders and to whom the leaders are, in one way or another, thoroughly responsible. To what extent such organizations will be necessary in the reconstituted diocese remains to be seen. Yet, given diocesan federations of Catholic Action, diocesan youth organizations, diocesan Councils of men and women, they ought to be more representative (from the parish level up), and, also, responsible not so much to a bureaucrat as to a committee from the diocesan senate. Perhaps the democratically elected heads of diocesan-wide organizations could serve *ex officio* as members of the senate. It is axiomatic that unless such organizations have some room for responsible maneuverability and some freedom of action, they will attract little or no popular support and will fail in achieving their announced goals.

A more serious problem, however, is the question of the so-called unofficial organizations—the diocesan paper, the diocesan interracial councils, and other social action organizations which are "quasi-sponsored." Many such structures would like to live in the best of all possible worlds, being "official" enough to speak for the Church in some fashion but "unofficial" enough not to be under the complete control of the bishop or the chancery. Logically speaking, such organizations seem to be contradictions: they are either official or they are not. If they are, they act as an arm of the bishop; and if they are not, they cannot claim to speak for the diocese or the Church, but only for themselves. However, in practice, such organizations can be extraordinarily helpful—they can represent the Church's official concern about a given matter, without necessarily committing the Church to a specific position (by "Church" we here mean the official hierarchy of the Church). Such quasi-sponsored organizations can do an effective and important work as go-between for the Church in extremely complicated social issues. But they can operate successfully in delicate border areas only if there is confidence and trust between the official Church structure and the staff workers of the organization. However, since such an organization functions largely in complicated and emotion-laden areas of activity, and since its staff members frequently must make quick and difficult decisions, there is almost automatic tension between it and the official diocesan structure. Probably this will continue even when the diocese is reconstituted on a more representative and professional basis, but the tensions, in our judgment, are well worth the price.

In addition to the official and quasi-official organizations, we now see emerging, all over the country, the independent organizations—associations of laymen which have come into being, at least in part, because of dissatisfaction with the representativeness and the effectiveness of official diocesan organizations. Even though part of the motivation of such groups is anti-clerical and some of the people involved in forming them often act like members of the lunatic fringe, there is no question that such groups have an important role to play in the future of the Church, as pressure groups working within the Church to promote reform, and as completely unofficial and non-ecclesiastical associations of Christian laymen concerned with the problems of the Christian implications for contemporary life.

In the beginning the official organizations may have more appeal, but as the diocesan structure modernizes itself to permit a direct representative participation of laymen in the government of the diocese, the strictly non-ecclesiastical, independent organizations will probably increase in membership. One must also recognize the possibility of a kind of federation of New Communities, constituting yet another kind of unofficial lay organization within the diocese.

It would seem very likely also that new trans-parochial or extra-parochial structures will emerge which will represent some kind of combination of the functions of the parish and diocesan organizations. They will be like the parish in that they will probably be liturgically oriented and will strive for a communitarian ethos; and they will resemble diocesan associations in that they will be organized around some special activities and will recruit membership from all parts of the diocese. One presumes that such groupings, generally with special priests assigned to cooperate with them, will come into being to serve Christians involved in specific kinds of work, like the arts and communication, the secular university, government, hospital work, and perhaps business. How official such groups will be will probably depend both on the people involved and on the common interests that brought them together.

It should be clear from the preceding paragraphs that the diocese we are describing would be much less easy to outline on an organizational chart than the current type of diocese. Staff officers, diocesan senates and assemblies, official and quasi-official organizations, unofficial organizations, new communities, functional groupings, parishes, extra-parochial and trans-parochial organizations, centralized and decentralized agencies—all these suggest chaos, at least to anyone who demands neat organizational lines.

If it is chaotic, it will be a constantly shifting chaos, as new combinations are tried and discarded, and old groupings are reorganized and given new tasks. And while it may not look as efficient as the present diocese, we believe it will actually prove more efficient, because a complex and flexible organizational structure can more easily cope with the complicated and ever changing problems the Church must face in an urban environment. The structures we have described will allow for experimentation and innovation, a feature which is absolutely imperative for progress. Any large corporate body which does not wish to grow stagnant and stale must be able to cope organizationally with a wide variety of different subgroups, operating with relative autonomy and perhaps even in competition. Such a structure does not look neat on a chart, but the world in which we live isn't very neat either. And we submit that the pastor of the diocese ought to be more concerned with vitality, flexibility, and innovation within the ecclesiastical structures than with orderly organizational charts.

No particular pastoral form can successfully claim to be the only *really* Catholic structure or the only way that *really* priestly work can be done. The parish has made this claim in the past and still makes it. Such a claim is patently absurd, and neither the Church nor the priesthood ought to be limited to the neighborhood area, by either ecclesiastical or sociological theorizing. One presumes that the

Church and the priesthood are wherever Christian people are gathered together with religious concerns, and in the absence of far more research on effectiveness than is presently likely to be done, any claim to be "more effective" made by any single ecclesiastical form of organization, cannot be sustained.

Two final questions must be discussed. It is frequently asserted that one area of the city is more important than another, in the work of the Church. We are told by some, for example, that the inner city or the poverty areas have the most claim on diocesan effort. In some ways, such an assertion is true; poverty areas, in terms of both charity and justice, ought to be subsidized financially and ought to have high claim on the services of skillful personnel. Certainly, service to the poor is one of the elements of the very definition of the Christian Church. But there are other forms of poverty in the world besides material poverty, and the central city has by no means a monopoly on human suffering. However, the question of whether there is more suffering in the central city or the suburbs, from the point of view of the Church's work in the diocese, is quite irrelevant. The diocese is not a part of the city, it includes the whole city; and it can work effectively in one area only if it works effectively in all areas. The problems of the inner city will never be resolved, either on the political or the human level, without the cooperation of those who do *not* live in the inner city.

And the larger question of the quality of life in a metropolis will be solved in suburbia, if it is solved at all. Any approach to the work of the Church in the metropolis which attempts to concentrate on one particular solution or area, and ignores the complex challenges of the metropolitan area, is a narrow, rigid, and ultimately self-defeating approach. Those who affirm that the inner city, or suburbia, or the university is "where the action is" are speaking the truth only if they recognize that there is very important action in all areas of the city, and that the Church belongs wherever the city is.

Finally, the diocese, if it is large enough, must concern itself with division and sub-division. Whether major American archidioceses can be divided into several independent dioceses depends to a considerable extent, one supposes, on the history, geography, and social structure of their metropolitan region. The Catholic Church within the city of New York, for example, functions with relative effectiveness in two dioceses, and could perhaps include several more dioceses within its present boundaries. On the other hand, it is difficult to see how the city of Chicago could be divided into two dioceses. Thus, there are no simple answers to the question of whether new dioceses ought to be formed, or whether old dioceses ought to be divided into vicariates. Nor are there simple answers as to how the lines of division should be drawn, though it ought to be clear that great care should be exercised in setting up new sub-structures, and that to do so without the most competent professional advice could be criminally negligent.

Several points might be noted, however. There should be as much social heterogeneity as possible in a diocese or a vicariate, so that priests and people do not become too closely identified with any single social class or set of human problems and needs. It also does not seem equitable for one diocese to have but few financial problems, while its next-door neighbor, part of the same metropolitan region, is overwhelmed with financial difficulties. Clearly, too, a segregated diocese would be a tragic mistake.

We also must realize that, beyond a certain number of parishes, the span of control is simply too great for one administrator to cope with, at least if he is to be reasonably familiar with the problems of his parishes. Exactly what the limit ought to be for the number of Catholic parishes in a diocese cannot be affirmed with confidence. Five hundred parishes under one man and one central office are too many, but perhaps one hundred are too many too, and perhaps even thirty parishes are too many for one bishop to effectively supervise and inspire. We simply do not know, though given the large number of dioceses in the country, research in this matter ought to be feasible. Whether a limitation on the number should involve the creation of new dioceses or merely the formation of vicariates and sub-vicariates, is a question the response to which will vary from city to city, although much is to be said for having some kind of metropolitan ecclesiastical authority which is at least roughly coterminous with urban or metropolitan divisions.

The author writes these pages on the sociology of the diocese with grave misgivings and reservations. There is so much to be done before the organizational Church can be a supple enough instrument to deal with the problems of the metropolis, and so little hope of its being done. Diocesan construction will be reformed eventually, but, one suspects, only in response to overwhelming pressure from dissatisfied laity and clergy, and the inexorable growth of metropolitan problems. Much talent, energy, enthusiasm, and goodwill is likely to be wasted before such reorganization occurs.

But we may hope that the new diocese which emerges in the next quarter of a century will not quickly become so rigid and inflexible, and that another generation will not be faced with the same problem as this one—the problem of an urban Church which, quite publicly, is tripping over its own feet.

III
THE CHURCH AND ITS PEOPLE

10 *The Formation of a Christian*

Sociologists use the word "socialization" to indicate the process by which a person learns the kind of behavior expected of him in the social context in which he finds himself. Through this process he learns the norms, values, and role expectations of his culture. The primary socializing influence is, of course, the family. The most important part of the socialization experience takes place in the very early years, perhaps even before a person is seven years old, although various elements of the socialization process (one's job or political association, for example) go on in young adulthood, and the process of learning expected behavior never really stops until death.

It is important to note that the socialization experience is, for the most part, informal. One learns the behavior and the attitudes that are appropriate for one's social role mostly by imitation. Formal instruction, either in the schoolroom or from one's elders, generally plays a minor, though occasionally a relatively important part, in the socialization process.

From the point of view of the sociologist, what is frequently called "Christian formation" is really "religious socialization," the process by which the human being acquires the values, norms, and behavioral expectations for the religious dimension of his life, and indeed learns which dimensions of life may be considered "religious," and which are exempted from religious influence. The primary religious socializers are parents. The child's religious attitudes and behavior are shaped so strongly by his family experience that it is only with extraordinary difficulty that the family impact can be altered; and the family, in turn, is both directly and indirectly influenced by the social class to which it belongs.

Certain kinds of religious behavior are expected of different classes within ethnic groups, and the child quickly learns from his parents what "our kind of people" do in religious matters. The upper middleclass tend to be active church members; the lower middleclass and upper working class are largely devout, hard-working, but docile church-goers, while the lower working class, at least in many countries and some American ethnic groups, is religiously indifferent. The upper class is church-affiliated but politely skeptical. The intellectuals, of course, hold to their established faith of bourgeois agnosticism. By the time the child comes into any direct contact with his religious group, his orientations toward religion have been rather well formed, and, as we have noted frequently before, it is extraordinarily naive to expect that formal religion can produce any significant religious socialization experience, whether by formal education, worship, or "instant religious experience." None of these notably change the religious orientations of most people.

It follows from this, as we have suggested before, that the wise pastoral worker concentrates his efforts on those whose previous religious socialization is such that it at least leaves them open to further socialization, if it does not incline them toward it. It may seem harsh to stress that the vast majority of church-goers have been so shaped by their early religious socialization that churches can have little influence on them, but the theoretical and empirical evidence to this effect is overwhelming. One will occasionally encounter dedicated and enthusiastic Christians whose background would have inclined them either to indifference or to bourgeois piety, but these are exceptions; and at least in the present state of our knowledge of socialization in general and of religious socialization in particular, we cannot expect to elicit enthusiastic religious dedication among those whose previous religious experience does not prepare them for further socialization. Thus, it is precisely those from already good Catholic families who are likely to be more influenced by Catholic schools. It is those families with a metropolitan outlook who will prove to be metropolitan Christians. It is from those families where religion is viewed non-instrumentally that we can expect more non-instrumental people. And if human progress requires that we chip away patiently at the apathetic, indifferent, "instrumental" masses, this is much more likely to succeed through the work of an elite laity than through the direct efforts of the pastoral worker.

External forms of behavior can be changed. Some of the

evidence available in the NORC* study of Catholic schools leads us to conclude that when young people from families that are not particularly devout are in Catholic high schools, their religious behavior is substantially better than that of their families and as good as that of youngsters from devout Catholic families; but shortly after their departure from school, their religious behavior reverts to that which had been established for them as normative in their own family. Similarly, the patterns of behavior learned in the novitiate experience, at the beginning of the religious life, will be sustained as long as the individual is living in the religious community, subject to the considerable pressures and sanctions which are inevitably brought to bear to assure such behavior. This does not mean, however, that new norms or values have been acquired; it simply means that repetition and sanctions enforce desirable behavior, without necessarily changing internal attitudes, or at least without changing them very much.

It might be concluded from the previous paragraphs that we must despair of substantial religious development and change after the age of seven among those who are not prepared for it in their family milieu. While "despair" is too strong a word, and while we must constantly strive to improve our techniques, still, speaking realistically, we have no reason to be very optimistic.

With these cautions in mind, how are we to go about the formation of a Christian? The first step is to discover what

* The National Opinion Research Center (University of Chicago), of which the author is Program Director (1968).

a person's needs, aspirations, and values are. It will do no good to tell him what he ought to be or what he ought to be doing. We must first discover who he is and who he hopes to be, and then show him how commitment to Christianity will enable him to move from where he is to where he wants to be. Since most people have several different and often conflicting self-images and constellations of aspirations, the Christianity presented to a person need not coincide with all his aspirations and the totality of his self-image. It is sufficient that it appeal to him enough to move him at least to investigate further.

In human history, the principal needs to which man's religion has responded are his needs for meaning and for belonging, for an explanation of the diverse and conflicting experiences he has in life, and for assurance that he faces life and its problems and hopes, not by himself, but in communion with others. Moreover, perhaps at no time more than our own has the need for meaning and belonging been felt so intensely and so explicitly, and it is for this reason that we stress so often the crucial role that the small religious group plays in the pastoral work of the Church. It is in this group that man will come to know the Church as responding to his needs if he comes to know it at all. Religious formation does not proceed, except in very rare instances, on an individual basis. Socialization takes place in a person as part of a community; effective religious socialization, in one who is part of a reasonably small religious community. Thus, the prudent pastoral worker will either find a preexisting community with which he can work, or he will set in motion forces to create a community

with which he can work, because without community man
is not socialized.

It must be stressed that religious socialization is, for
most people, a long, slow and gradual process. New patterns of behavior are not acquired overnight, nor are old
patterns deepened and enriched in one instant experience.
Violence can be done to the human personality to produce
new kinds of behavior almost instantaneously, but this sort
of religious electro-shock therapy, whether in a novitiate, a
retreat, or a cursillo, manipulates man, treats him like a
vegetable, but does not respect his needs, his dignity, or
the organic principles of human growth.

And so the pastoral worker cannot expect change overnight. He cannot assume that even a group of reasonably
open, reasonably well-intentioned, but somewhat apathetic and passive Christians, in the space of one meeting
or two, or even after a year or two years of meetings, will
develop into the kind of "militants" of which some French
writings speak so frequently. (He may also be well-advised
to be skeptical of how militant the French militants are
and of how many remain so.)

It follows that religious formation will require much
reassurance because not only will the pastor grow discouraged with the slow pace of progress but so will his followers. To respect the gradual nature of growth and at the
same time to spur others on to ever greater growth requires a delicate balance and a pastor who is neither indifferent nor too supportive. As a matter of fact, it is most
unlikely that the pastor can play this role in religious formation unless powerful ties of personal friendship develop
between himself and his followers. Thus the constant de-

mand of the new breed that their priests love them and
that they be permitted to love their priests in return,
shows a great deal of psychological wisdom.

There must also be action in the formation experience.
The Cardijn formula—Observe, Judge, Act—is in complete accord with what we know of the psychology and
sociology of human growth. Man deepens his perspective,
broadens his horizons, enriches his personality, by engaging in a constant dialectic between thought and action. If
one or the other is deficient, growth will be abortive. But
granted that Cardijn's steps are psychologically correct, it
does not follow that they have always been used with dis-
cretion or intelligence. The conviction in many of the
Catholic Action organizations in the United States that the
process must occur on a fixed night every two weeks is
mechanistic in the extreme. This search for "action" every
two weeks in many a Catholic Action group would be
ludicrous if it were not so pathetic. Action should flow
from thought and lead to further thought, but not necessarily on a fixed bi-monthly schedule. Often there must be
much thought and dialogue before action can begin.

Formation, then, requires careful choice of personnel,
intensive training, group involvement, honest dialogue,
pastoral support, and, eventually, practical action. Even
under ideal circumstances, the problems will be great, and
the failures many. The danger of manipulation, the temptation to mass-produce apostles, the pitfalls of ill-founded
enthusiasm are not easily avoided. If only there were as
many magic answers as generations of eager seminarians
have confidently believed they possessed!

A final note should be added on the formational experience of a Christian. It should be joyous; it should even be fun. It seems to be almost a law of human behavior that the more important a matter is, the more likely people are to add a saving dash of play or humor, after Chesterton's wise adage that "life is too serious to be taken seriously." An atmosphere devoid of playfulness and sport cannot expect to evoke consistently the most adequate human response. One is compelled to observe that the most serious fault besetting formational efforts within American Catholicism has been the absence of such human playfulness. Unlike buffoonery or defensive irony, this is a profoundly Christian virtue. Who can doubt that when their eyes were opened, the disciples going to Emmaus smiled so broadly that it all turned into joyous laughter?

And who can think the Stranger did not join in?

11 The Church and Young People

There is no more appealing and frustrating aspect of pastoral work than dealing with young people. Adolescents are, of course, vivacious, responsive, quick to give their affection and loyalty; but they are also undependable, mercurial, and just as quick to withdraw their loyalty. But the worst thing about adolescents is that they grow up and become not the dedicated, enthusiastic Christians the pastoral workers would wish, but narrow, staid adults not unlike their parents.

Adolescence is perhaps the last period of life when one can reasonably expect a major increment in the individual's personality constellation. During the years of the identity-intimacy crises, to use Erik Erikson's term, a person may still expand the dimensions of his personality beyond the limits imposed by his family, his social class, and his culture; but after college graduation, such change is extremely unlikely to occur. It is a critical period—perhaps the most critical period in one's life—and for all the time and effort poured into youth work, if one were to examine results, one might conclude that the Church has been conspicuously unsuccessful.

Some sociologists, such as James Coleman, contend that the adolescent period in American society is so intense that it actually represents a separate culture with different values, roles and norms in its pattern of behavior than the adult culture. These observers argue that adolescent behavior is determined to a considerable extent by the values of the peer group, which are at variance with the values of the larger society.

Other researchers discovered, however, that the peer group exercises an even more powerful tyranny during the pre-teen years, and that throughout adolescence, the values of young people progressively become more like those of their parents. Whether adolescent society is a separate culture from the viewpoint of the pastoral worker, is not as important as the simple fact that the world of adolescence is quite different from the world of parents, and that many of the values to be found in adolescent society are either different from, or are caricatures of, adult values.

The peer group has fantastic power, exercised in a more obvious and direct fashion than power in the world of adults. It is a world of fierce competition and great unhappiness, punctuated periodically by bursts of euphoric "fun"; it is a world of seemingly very deep friendships formed quickly, and shattered quickly. There is great fear and curiosity, and great uncertainty, about sex. With its aggressiveness and shyness, hope and fear, loneliness and desperate conformity, the adolescent world requires the pastoral worker who wishes to have any influence in it, to understand it thoroughly, sympathize with it, and even to some extent, to learn to think as its inhabitants do.

However, he must also be wary of the danger of over-acculturation. Most adults make no attempt to understand teen culture and are viewed, implicitly, at least, as enemies. Moreover, the adolescent's need for adult friendship is so great that the pastoral worker who seems sympathetic and understanding is warmly welcomed, so warmly in fact that, unless he is a stable, unalienated person, he may find himself "going native" and becoming a teen-ager himself. This danger is enhanced if his own training did not permit him to develop his personality beyond that of a psychological adolescent. As David Riesman has wittily pointed out: adolescence is bad enough the first time through; to have to live it twice would be unbearable!

The second observation that must be made, at least about middle-class teen-agers, is that many if not most of them are obsessed by self-hatred. The use of love as a means to obtain satisfactory performance is so widespread in American society that most middle-class young people do not seem to experience enough unconditioned love during their early years to be able to accept themselves as worthwhile, lovable human beings. Indeed, for middle-class youth, much of the seemingly delinquent behavior in which they engage is a form of self-punishment in which they release their aggressions toward themselves for their own worthlessness, and toward their parents for having made them worthless. Self-hatred is made particularly intense by the loneliness of the teen years, when a young person literally has no one he can trust, no one with whom he can communicate his own feeling of emptiness, no one who will be able to tell him that most other adolescents have the same feelings—a bit of information that brings tremendous solace, for if one is not the only one who feels worthless, there may still be some hope.

The adolescent years are times when the young person is developing and testing his skills. He wishes, at least on occasion, to push his abilities as far as he can to find out exactly what his limitations are. This is a time when challenges which force him to strain and test his skills is extremely important, although curiously enough, in American society we do very little to present challenge to teenagers, apart from what seems to him to be dull and irrelevant academic work. The need for developing competence, therefore, is side-tracked into unproductive areas, such as the pursuit of knowledge about automobiles, rock-and-roll music, and the lives of Hollywood personalities. Society permits the teen-ager to be a specialist in nothing else, and so he becomes a specialist in trivia.

The young person attempts to fashion for himself, particularly in the later teen years, an ideology, a world view, a series of answers to the basic questions of who he is, what life is for, and what satisfactions he expects out of life. As Erik Erikson has pointed out, ideology and identity go hand in hand, and the crisis of ideology is virtually the same as the crisis of identity. Traditional religions are of singularly little use to most adolescents in fashioning their own personal ideology, partly because the representatives of their religious group show little understanding of, or sympathy for adolescents, and partly because religion, and indeed God himself, are part of another world, one which the teen-ager deeply resents. God becomes identified with his father and the Church with his mother, and the adolescent is strongly inclined, at least much of the time, not to like either of these pair. Most of the so-called religious crises of young adulthood have very little to do with questions of doctrine, and very much to do with the transference of resentments from one's parents to God and the Church (a rather bad deal for organized religion). But it must be admitted that the behavior of many religious functionaries who work with young people has provided at least ample opportunity for young people to turn organized religion into their handy all-purpose ogre.

Take, for example, the rather frequent attempts to argue or threaten the young person out of his "crisis" obsession. When "crisis of faith" is properly understood, it has nothing to do with belief, but is rather a psychological and personality problem. It is, in fact, a demand for sympathy and love, not for argumentation, though the young person is, in some perverse way, pleased by argumentation, because it confirms him in his suspicion that neither church nor churchmen love him.

In the later years of adolescence, the young person is seeking intimacy, friendship, and love, and in the process must overcome the abiding distrust he has learned from his family and peer group environment. It is not an easy task, and many young people do not seem to be very successful at it. While they do form friendships and eventually marry, interpersonal behavior is never free from distrust and self-rejection, and the amount of happiness they achieve in life, to say nothing of the amount of service they are able to render, is severely limited. What they need from adults is both guidance and friendship—guidance which does not demand obedience, and friendship which does not demand development according to the dictates of the adult.

There is relatively little such guidance and friendship in the lives of most young Americans. Perhaps at some later stage of development of the human race, the relationship between parents and their teen-age offspring will be different than it is today, but parents have so much emotional energy invested in the young person's being "a credit" to the family that they are not well equipped psychologically to facilitate his growth to free and autonomous adulthood. There is much tragedy in the collapse of communication between young people and their parents, communication which may or may not be reestablished on some more mature level later in life. But anyone who has had an opportunity to watch closely the exploitation of a child and his emotions by parents, particularly in the middle-class culture, is forced to conclude that most parents get exactly what they deserve.

These findings about the sociology and social psychology of adolescence engender a number of pertinent pastoral corollaries:

1. The pastoral worker will have little effectiveness if he attempts to work with isolated individuals. He must either capture a whole group of teen-agers or he will capture no one.

2. He must resign himself to unfair criticism of his

efforts. The teen-ager's need of a scapegoat is so strong that any attention a pastoral worker may show to one person or to one group will immediately be labelled "favoritism" by others. It is quite impossible for the pastoral worker to so apportion his time that each adolescent or group receives an exactly equal amount of attention. Even if he could do this, it would be foolish to attempt it, because some teen-agers have more need of his services, while others represent greater opportunity for his work. Nobody engaged in pastoral work with any age level is going to please everybody, but this is particularly true when one works with teen-agers, and it is folly to try.

3. Teen-agers are adults in-the-making, and the pastoral worker must respect this adulthood in his dealing with them. He must never act without consulting them; he must never try to deceive them, or deal behind their back; he must get their viewpoint on all the major problems of their activities; he must never lecture them or pontificate over them. Further, he must frequently resist parental pressure to divert his efforts for parental purposes. From the teen-agers' viewpoint, this would be a betrayal and would completely destroy their confidence in him. It is not easy to treat adolescents with adult respect, particularly since, in many instances, they are not capable of responding like adults. But if a pastoral worker expects to approach teen-agers on terms of reciprocal justice, he may just as well spare himself the inevitable disappointment.

4. While social and recreational activities may serve some purpose, particularly in those areas where they are not provided by other agencies, the most effective kind of

pastoral work with teen-agers involves challenging their generosity and providing the materials from which they can fashion an ideology and thus an identity. The challenge of ideas and altruistic service are not only far more effective religiously than the challenge of athletics and dances; they are also much more in keeping with the needs and problems of middle-class teen-agers. Small discussion and interaction groups may not attract nearly so many people as a dance or a basketball game, but the pastoral worker is deceiving himself if he thinks that a large crowd at a dance is proof that he has real influence with teen-agers.

5. The Catholic liturgy, as we have seen, can provide extremely meaningful religious experience for a teen-age group, particularly when the group has the satisfaction of engaging in a common project, although it must be admitted that the Roman liturgy as it is generally performed in this country produces nothing for the teen-age population but sheer boredom.

6. The most important function of the pastoral worker in the life of an adolescent is to love him and reassure him that he is lovable. This may not seem obvious at first because many middle-class teen-agers have a veneer of poise and sophistication, a pose of "coolness" which would make it appear that they have little doubt about themselves and have complete confidence in everything they do. Most of this is sham. The uncertainties, doubts, and anguishes of adolescent life are probably tormenting even the poised and seemingly mature young person. To be reassured, to be told one is good, that one has ability and promise, that one can indeed have a happy life—these things may seem to

the pastoral worker so obvious that they hardly need saying, and so easy to say that they hardly seem important. And yet it is the most important thing that religion, the Church, and the pastoral worker can do for a young person, and also the most effective way of practicing Christian charity in the teen-age world. It is not very difficult, but in its absence, most other forms of pastoral work will have only perfunctory success, and in its presence, many traditional forms of pastoral work will prove quite unimportant, indeed.

There is, of course, a problem in loving adolescents and in permitting them to love you—the problem of transference, or, in less Freudian terminology, the teen-age crush, and the pastoral worker may just as well resign himself to being the object of such "crushes" from members of both sexes. Especially for the Catholic pastoral worker, so indoctrinated in the dangers of human affection, to be an object of such a crush can be a very distressing experience, one that can tempt him to flee from the adolescent. But such flight is, in itself, immature, and a betrayal of the young person's trust. The wise and discreet pastoral worker treats the affection of an adolescent with gentleness, humor, and respect. He understands that such bursts of affection are part of growing up, and does not consider them a threat either to his vocation or to his chastity. Obviously, a reasonable amount of self-possession is necessary in such circumstances, but then one who lacks this should not be working with teen-agers in the first place.

It is possible, of course, for some of these crushes to mature into adult friendships as the years go on, and the pastoral worker is surely grateful when this happens. But he does not attempt to maneuver the relationship in that direction. His principal aim is that the teen-ager may grow to adulthood, simultaneously free and mature, open and dedicated to the work of the Church and the work of mankind. It is perhaps cruel to say it, but in his relationship with the pastoral worker, the teen-ager should find the freedom, guidance, support, and love which he usually looks for in vain in his relationship with his parents.

Virtually everything we have said in Chapter V, on "Community in the Church," is relevant to the teen-age community. Theirs is an unstable, transitory community, but while it exists it is a powerful one. Of itself, it is neither good nor bad, although generally it is at variance with the goals of adult society. It does not follow, however, that it need be at variance with the goals of the Church. The wise pastoral worker looks on the teen-age clique, not as a band of ruffians or pagans, nor as a group of rebels, but as potential allies, because many of the things that teen-agers reject in adult culture, he rejects, too.

We have said virtually nothing in this chapter about juvenile delinquency, even though there is a vast sociological literature on the subject. We do not intend to deny the reality of the problem, nor to imply that pastoral workers can make no contribution in dealing with it. But, unfortunately, most juvenile delinquents are beyond the reach of all but a very few highly skilled workers, and even here the problems are usually so great that no very great success is to be expected. The delinquent must be helped, but the real concern of the pastoral worker should be the non-delinquent adolescent.

12 The Church and Women

Through its long history Catholicism has maintained a double standard for women, and the situation has become particularly acute in our own age. Pope John's endorsement of feminism in the encyclical *Pacem in Terris* provided the green light for those within the Church who had long felt that the equal rights movement was just as relevant inside the Church as outside it.

Women are still, at least in theory, second-class citizens in the Church. For example, the rights of nuns in Canon Law are very meagre; they have no effective representation in the Congregation of Religious which presides over the destiny of the female religious of the world, and their only voice at Vatican Council II was a handful of observers.

By both Canon Law and ecclesiastical tradition, women in the Church are subject to men. Even a woman who has tremendous responsibility in her religious community, college, or hospital is still expected to show a respectful, if not obsequious attitude toward the men who are technically her employees, but who actually view themselves as the bishop's representatives in supervising the religious community. No nation in the modern world has as little regard for the rights of women as does the Catholic Church.

Further, what has come to be considered the Catholic philosophy toward women is strongly familistic. Generations of young Catholic girls have been taught that a woman's place is in the home, and that a woman's only true satisfactions will come from the successful fulfillment of the role of wife and mother. Indeed, frequently her mentors have insisted that the more often she bears a child, the better Christian woman she is.

It ought to be noted that this is not, in fact, Catholic doctrine. It is merely an historical accretion to Catholic teaching which reflected the type of culture the Church was working in. It had little to do with the Gospel's view of women or with the Christian teaching of the equality of all human beings in the sight of God.

And, sad to say, many priests and ecclesiastical leaders have been and still are exploitative in their attitude toward women, largely, at least, because they need to avoid the amenities and personal, human manner which could betray their fear of women.

But this is only one aspect of the Catholic Church's attitude toward women, although it is one which is very frequently encountered. Whatever Canon Law may say or have said, women have consistently played important roles in the history of the Church, and some of them, like St. Catherine of Sienna, have not hesitated to rebuke even Popes. The mitered abbesses of the Middle Ages ruled great monastery estates. Today, nuns who are college presidents, hospital administrators, and religious superiors have far more power *in practice* than most other women, even those in responsible positions in the secular, business, and academic world. It is surely not an exaggeration to say that the majority of U.S. women college presidents are nuns, and that these women probably exercise greater actual power within the Catholic Church than women exercise in any other major American religious denomination. But there is urgent need for legal, statutory guarantee of their powers and (especially) of the rights of their very numerous "subjects."

Anti-feminism in the Church developed through certain well-defined historical causes. For a thousand years Catholicism upheld the Christian doctrine that there was neither "male nor female, Jew nor gentile, Greek nor Roman" in the eyes of Christ Jesus, a doctrine which most historians on the subject are inclined to agree created the atmosphere of respect for women in which the feminist movement could begin—an atmosphere which existed in no other culture in the world, except the Christian. That the Catholic Church failed to follow its own insight to its logical conclusion must be rated as one of the great tragedies of its history.

First of all, the legal structure and governance of the Church have historically been Latin, and the Reformation removed much of the non-Latin, northern European influence from the Church. Whether because of the tradition of the Teutonic tribes or the development of Anglo-Saxon law, or the more rapid progress of political democracy in Protestant nations, it does seem that the non-Latin elements in Western Christianity were quicker to develop a culture in which it was possible to think of women as equal to men, and not as second-class citizens. Even today feminism is quite weak in most Latin countries, and the partnership approach to the relationship between the sexes has been very slow in developing there.

Then too, ecclesiastical celibacy, not so much in itself, but through the type of training that was deemed necessary to support it, has developed in many clerics a fear and suspicion of women. Woman was viewed as a temptation, a threat, something that one had to master if one was not to be mastered. Obviously, many priests or bishops rose above such training, but no one who lived in a seminary even as recently as fifteen years ago would deny that this attitude was widespread. It is surely not an attitude conducive to dealing with woman as a partner or an equal.

Finally, the Church absorbed too much of the rural values of its past, and became too immersed in a culture which was not flexible enough to keep pace with the rapid changes in the modern world. The equality of woman is largely an urban phenomenon. The Church, at least until very recently, has been fondly attached to rural customs and has tried, in many countries, unsuccessfully, to transplant these rural values into an urban context.

The question of the origin of the anti-feminist spirit in the Church is obviously much more complex than this brief sketch has indicated. (One need only look at Ireland, a country apparently dominated by its women and its priests, to note that within the Catholic tradition there are wide variations in the status of women.)

But the feminist movement has at last emerged, and emerged strongly, in the Church. Many liberal American Catholics seem to be obsessed with the question of the ordination of women. Obviously this problem is one that is going to have to be resolved with something more than the assertion that the Church has never ordained women in the past and cannot do so now. Besides being somewhat irrelevant, this is an assertion that may not be true, since historical research seems to indicate that the deaconesses of the early Church were, in fact, considered to be in sacred orders.

But if the problem of the ordination of women must be resolved, it is clear that it is not likely to be resolved in the immediate future, and that more critical issues must be faced long before the Church can seriously consider the ordination of women. Presumably the pastoral worker is sophisticated enough to realize that differential psychology and biology have established that woman is not constitutionally inferior to man and that, with the exception of specifically sexual functions, there is little innate difference in their abilities or inclinations. Most differences which have, in fact, emerged, are cultural and are learned, rather than inherited.

Presumably, too, the pastoral worker will be aware that in modern marriage women are not subject to their husbands, nor for that matter, ideally, are husbands subject to their wives. In the modern family there is a division in the use of authority, the husband being responsible for certain kinds of decision-making, the wife responsible for other areas, and a third area in which the decisions are made jointly. Furthermore, there is considerable variety among families in drawing the precise lines of this three-fold division of authority.

It has frequently been urged that this modern stress on partnership in marriage is at variance with the traditional Christian ideal, even as the high rate of divorce flatly contradicts it. Adequate discussion of these questions would range far beyond the purpose of this book. But we would cite one sociological finding which is of some importance to the pastoral worker: there is overwhelming evidence that modern marriages which *do prove stable* are demonstrably much happier and much more fulfilling than were stable marriages of the past. In other words, couples who *are* "happily married" today are much *more* happily married than happily married couples used to be.

But the critical problem for the Church is not so much changing the thinking of some of its leaders about marriage or about the "natural" role of women. These ideas are headed for the graveyard of the past, in any case. The critical question for the Church, at least at the present time, is two-fold. First, is the Church willing to follow the lead of Pope John in campaigning for equality of opportunity, rights, and representation for women everywhere in the world? Secondly, is the Church willing to concede this equality to women within its own structure? Masculine exploitation and the double standard still exist in most countries, and are an increasingly unbearable tyranny for educated, sophisticated, modern women. Both justice and realism demand that the Church join the crusade to secure full justice for women. Indeed, the Church should be just as committed to this crusade as it should be to that for interracial justice.

But such a commitment would be utterly worthless unless, within its own boundaries, it is prepared to practice what it preaches; unless, for example, the parish school is really run by the professional women who staff it, instead of by the pastor who feels that his masculinity would be diminished if he were not the administrator, even though he may have no professional training for it. Again, is the Church willing to eliminate the practice whereby highly trained professional nuns are still required to do menial work because a fantastic sense of economy thinks this is a way of saving money? Is the Church willing to give nuns adequate representation in all its institutions—parish, councils, dioceses, and senates—on up to and including the supreme administrative bodies of the Church? Is the Church willing to reorganize relationships between priests and nuns at the parish level so that they are equal partners working as a team, communicating in a thoroughly professional fashion, instead of behaving like threatened, insecure rivals? We hardly need add that such neurotic relationships are anything but a sign of that unity and love by which all men may identify the disciples of Christ!

The feminist movement will go ahead with or without the Church. Even though it has but tender roots in most nations of the world, it is likely to grow rapidly in the years immediately ahead. The Church has lost many splendid opportunities to provide leadership for the pilgrimage of man in the last half millennium; to miss this opportunity would be tragically stupid, particularly in view of the Church's long history of giving power, responsibility, and leadership to women, at least in practice if not in theory. The Church will have a long task ahead if it means to put its house in order. There is bad seminary training based on bad ideology at the root of the feminist dilemma in the Church, as well as outmoded structures. The shape of the new training is only beginning to emerge.

There are surely no grounds for easy optimism about the problem of women in the Church. A younger generation of priests and seminarians will probably be far more open and sympathetic toward the movement for equality for women than is the present leadership, but to wait for their ascendency may take a quarter of a century, and by that time it may be too late for the Church to catch up. At the present time, the question does not even seem to be seriously considered. Only an incurable optimist would not be seriously worried about the Church's capacity to cope with the feminist revolution.

13 The Church and Vocations

With little exaggeration it might be said that the most notable aftermath of the Second Vatican Council in the American Church has been the precipitous decline in religious and priestly vocations. Many of the positive results of the Council have been rather slow in developing, but this dramatic negative consequence has occurred with extraordinary speed. Some religious orders of women now have only one-fourth as many people joining them as they had even five years ago; a number of seminaries have closed down and others are seriously considering going out of business. Unless the trend is reversed, it is not at all inconceivable that the vocation shortage in the United States will become, in the not too distant future, as serious as it is in France.

Because it refuses to do research on any of its serious problems, American Catholicism has yet to produce reliable data to explain this dramatic drop in vocations. But at least three plausible hypotheses can be advanced.

The first is that the religious and priestly life no longer

appeals to young people. This explanation has been advanced both by those who are critical of the younger generation and by those who are favorably disposed to it. The critics say that young Americans lack the generosity, the enthusiasm, and the religious dedication required to devote one's whole life to the service of God and the Church. Defenders of young Americans argue that, with the appearance of the secular volunteer organizations, the new stress on the dignity and holiness of matrimony, the new understanding of the lay vocation, dedicated and enthusiastic young people no longer believe they need to become priests or nuns to serve the Church and their fellowmen, and indeed, are frequently persuaded that they can serve better in the lay state than in the clerical or religious state. But both the critics and defenders also point to the celibacy requirement as affecting young people's attitudes toward the religious life. The emphasis on self-fulfillment, particularly self-fulfillment through sexual love, is so strong in modern society that young people are very dubious about celibacy, particularly when it is clear that many celibates themselves have grave reservations about the choice they have made. The papal encyclical on celibacy, or at least the way the encyclical's impact filtered through to the public, did little to solve the problem.

One does not want to deny completely the merits of either version of this first explanation of the vocation problem. Surely the social factors it describes are at work. But they were at work before the Vatican Council, and while they might explain a slow decline in vocations, they can scarcely account for the fantastic decline of the last few years. For the influence of these factors to have accelerated so much, something else was required.

The second explanation finds the root of the decline of religious vocations in the public discussions of problems of priestly and religious life these last several years. Priests and nuns have left their vocations before, but rarely with the dramatic publicity, not to say, in a few instances, exhibitionism that has occurred with the new freedom that the Vatican Council has brought the American Church. Some critics deplore the spreading of so much dirty linen before the public eye, and particularly the youthful public eye, as in itself enough to discourage religious vocations. Others welcome these public revelations and say that now young people have a more complete and realistic notion of what the priestly or religious life is really like, and are not likely to entertain the old, naive expectations. One could also observe that the great concern with self and the conditions of one's own life in a number of the departing priests and nuns is usually unmatched by any notable concern for service of others. Their revelations do not present a particularly attractive picture of the average priest or religious. A sophisticated young person who reads the articles and books by dissatisfied and departing priests and sisters may readily conclude that too many priests and nuns lead selfish and immature lives, and he would want to have no close association with them.

Again, one does not want to reject this explanation completely. The collapse of the old caste differences between priests and laity have made possible much closer friendships, and thus a much clearer notion of what priests and religious are really like. Since many priests and nuns do not always live up to the ideal of the past, it would not be surprising if young people found themselves disillusioned with the potentialities of a religious vocation. Certainly anyone touring Catholic college campuses today is struck by the contempt which many of the more serious students have for the religious order that runs the college. Some individual priests and nuns are admired, but the community itself is viewed with disdain. Once again, we note that the forces making for this situation have been long at work; while they may partially account for the decline of religious vocations, they do not explain why the decline has accelerated so greatly in the past several years.

We turn, therefore, to a third explanation, which looks not so much to cultural change but to social structural changes within the religious communities and within the process of vocation recruitment. Research on the sociology of vocations indicates that in most instances the proximate reason for a young person's venturing into a seminary or a novitiate is personal contact with a priest or a nun, while the remote origins of the vocation are to be found, usually, in the atmosphere of the family life and in the general cultural orientations in which the young person is raised. A priest or nun, especially a young priest or nun with whom the potential recruit can identify, has been the decisive influence, however, in the final decision to give the religious or priestly life a try. This suggests that the reason the decline in vocations has been so dramatic is that, by and large, younger priests and religious have simply stopped recruiting. One can even say, at least on the basis of impressions, that they have actively discouraged vocations (whether intentionally or not) by realistically discussing with potential recruits the problems and difficulties of the priestly and religious life.

This greater candor is, in part, a response to the new passion for total honesty to be found in the younger generation. But a much more serious reason is that so many of the younger priests and nuns are far from being happy or assured in their own vocations. The revolution triggered by the Vatican Council has profoundly shaken the whole Church, bringing some confusion and uncertainty to most Catholics. But the priesthood and the religious life, which are much more directly affected by the upheaval in the Church, are experiencing uncertainty and instability within their ranks in an extraordinary degree. It is, therefore, not in the culture outside of the priestly and religious life that we must look for the cause of the dramatic drop in vocations, but within that life itself.

Whether the new generation of priests and nuns would have proceeded differently if there had not been a Vatican Council II is problematic. Surely they would have found the traditional servitude of seminary and novitiate harder to accept than did their predecessors, and they probably would have been much less enthusiastic vocation recruiters than the youthful clergy and religious of even a decade ago. The tremendous surge of questioning, probing, and doubting that has swept the Church as an inevitable part of the post-Vatican renewal, has made the problems of new-breed priests and religious more explicit, more intense, and hence has so aggravated the vocation problem that it is now a gigantic crisis.

If this analysis is correct, it would mean that the conciliar changes precipitated a problem which would have evolved in any event, more slowly through a decade or two. If so, this may have been extremely fortunate. A gradual decline in vocations could have been ignored until it was too late to take countermeasures, but the precipitate decline of the last few years simply cannot be ignored by reasonable and intelligent administrators. Counteraction is now far more likely to be taken.

No doubt there are additional social and cultural factors which contribute to the crisis. The increased education and professionalization of the Catholic population, and the decline of the importance of the ethnic loyalty factor among Catholics have contributed to a decline of automatic respect for the clergy. When the priest was virtually the only professional in the parish, he was necessarily accorded a high professional status. But now that the Catholic population is becoming upper middle-class, the parish abounds in highly trained professionals who are much less inclined to regard the priesthood as a high status profession, especially since the training and competency of the clergy leave much to be desired.

Furthermore, the authoritarianism and paternalism of the older clergy and religious, however appropriate or tolerable it may have been in an ethnic era, is completely unacceptable to Catholics of the younger generation. It is no longer a secret, finally, that life in a rectory or convent can be distinctly unpleasant, and that not a few such institutions are presided over by tyrants who are past masters of the psychological destruction of their charges. If it is obvious to young people and their parents that the younger clergy and religious are *not* busy trying to recruit their successors, it is just as obvious that many of the older clergy and religious, by their authoritarianism, paternalism, and even tyranny, and also frequently by their incompetence, have created an image of their status which is hardly very appealing, especially to youth.

If the analysis presented thus far is even roughly correct, it is obvious that the vocation problem is a complex one that will not easily be solved. Third-rate research projects, new vocation directors, high-pressure recruiting techniques, wringing of hands, or even burying one's head in the sand, are not likely to help very much. Bishops and religious superiors must face these harsh facts: the religious and priestly life has a poor image with young Americans; the most effective vocation recruiters have not only given up recruiting, but have contributed to the decline of the image; therefore, only a drastic change in the image of the priestly and religious life will successfully meet the vocation crisis.

But the *image* will not be changed effectively unless the *reality* of the life and the work of the priest and nun is dramatically updated. The religious must be unmistakably identified by the younger generation as people whose lives are characterized by freedom, initiative, responsibility, and relevancy. For weal or woe, most young women who might be inclined to the religious life today are not interested in spending their lives teaching in the Catholic schools, nor are most young men drawn to a life of routine cultic and fund-raising activities in all-white middle-class parishes.

To repeat, only a dramatic renewal of the priestly and religious life will even slow up the decline of vocations. Such renewal may offend many of the more conservative members of a diocese or religious order, but while compromise between the conservatives and the liberals may preserve the structure for a while, in the long run it will be disastrous, because any renewal that bends to placate conservatives will, one very much fears, greatly antagonize potential recruits—and recruiters. Unless the changes are profound, even shattering, the religious life as we now know it is doomed, and the shortage of priestly vocations will become painfully acute in the United States before the present century is over. One senses, in talking with some ecclesiastical leaders, that this alternative would be more acceptable to them than the kind of changes which are necessary. It often seems that they would sooner preside over the liquidation of their ecclesiastical structures than see them changed. If so, let the dead bury their dead!

When the American Church has been honestly renewed, there will be a dramatic increase in vocations, but such renewal is likely to be a quarter of a century off, and by that time vocations may, quite literally, be dried up. Such a painful event would be the judgment of the Holy Spirit, leveled against us for our failure to respond to his inspirations toward renewal. We have, in effect, alienated the best of our young people, because the atmosphere of narrowness, rigidity, authoritarianism, and selfishness which they experience in the Church simply disgust them.

True, there may be more in the Church than they see; there may still be flexibility, generosity, enthusiasm, ex-

citement, and challenge. But *if they do not see* these qualities, the reason may very well be that the opposite qualities
are still so powerful in the Church as to obscure the attractive qualities, and that many ecclesiastical leaders are so
terrified by the revolutionary forces released at the Council that they are afraid to look resolutely at the potential
and promise which the present crisis implies.

A different aspect of the vocation crisis is somewhat
more reassuring. In recent years the screening of candidates has been far more careful. While in some instances
the use of personality tests has been naive, even on occasion in violation of privacy, the use of such tests, and of
intensive interviews, and the insistence upon serious and
really knowledgeable recommendations, in place of vapid
formalities, have accounted for a general improvement in
the quality, if not the quantity of religious vocations. Such
screening is particularly important because a different
image of the religious life and the priestly life in some
quarters has apparently attracted a rather different kind of
young person.

When a religious vocation was viewed as a life marked
by order, submissiveness, stability, and rigidity, it attracted
precisely those young people whose personality needs are
such as to make them seek an authoritarian and passive
style of life. It hardly need be said that such recruits are
the last people the Church needs as religious functionaries
at the present time, and they should be vigorously screened
out. To anyone with vision, this transitional loss of numbers is a sound and necessary investment, however long-
term.

Among qualities needed in the new Church which is

emerging in our revolutionary era, the ability to assume initiative and responsibility is of critical importance for a priest or a nun, and the best training they can undergo is one that provides opportunities for them to behave in a responsible fashion. Indeed, a young person's reaction to situations in which he is required to be responsible provides the most effective kind of screening procedure at the present time. This is precisely the opposite of the training that was imparted in the past, when passivity and docility were valued far more than maturity and responsibility, and when, in fact, those who were mature and able to take initiative and act responsibly were heavily penalized for these qualities. As priest-psychologist Eugene Kennedy has remarked, "In many instances religious training is calculated to make sick people think they are healthy and healthy people think they are sick."

Similarly it is of critical importance to determine whether the candidate for the sisterhood or priesthood is skillful in personal behavior, including behavior toward members of the opposite sex. One must note once again that this is precisely the opposite of the traditional requirement in this regard. If the seminarian or scholastic got along well with lay people and did not feel threatened by laity of the opposite sex, he was viewed as a poor risk, while the aspirant who was inclined to socialize only with fellow religious or priests was viewed as an ideal candidate. It hardly need be added that the training which produced passive, docile priests and nuns who were ill at ease with any but fellow religious is one of the major causes of the vocation problem we now face.

We remind the reader that much of what is said in this chapter is speculation, gained indeed, from a sociological perspective, but without benefit of thorough, comprehensive research. Nor, we repeat, is research alone going to solve the vocation problem, particularly the kind of superficial research for which the American Church seems to have a predilection. But it is dubious that the problem will be solved without research. And no one who has had any dealings with the leadership of the American Church on the subject of research can be very optimistic that the necessary, first-rate research is going to be done. Increasingly, one may expect to hear the Holy Spirit turn from gentle breathing to large, exhausted groans!

IV
THE CHURCH AND THE FUTURE

14 The Parish of the Future

A decade ago any book written on the subject of pastoral sociology would have been principally concerned with the parish and how it might be restructured for maximum effectiveness. But the changes in the Church have forced us to face the fact that the parish is not only not the exclusive center of pastoral life but that it may need almost total transformation if it is to be effective even in those areas (such as family life and worship) in which it would be expected to be effective to an exceptional degree.

While it is certainly true that the restructured (or transformed) parish will not be the only pastoral agency of the Church, the parish of the future will continue to play an extremely important role in the Church's work. And while pastoral sociology would insist that the other efforts of the Church in a diocese must be reorganized before reorganization of the parish will have much meaning, nonetheless, if the parish does not undergo a radical transformation, the restructuring of the diocese itself will have little effect. Thus, the reorganization of the parish along the lines that sociology would deem most effective must be seen as part, though a critically important part, of the total reorganization of the Church's efforts.

The changes which are necessary in the parishes, however, are typical of what pastoral sociology would recommend for the other forms of pastoral activity. And so, a description of the parish of the future will appropriately summarize much of what has already been said in this book. We should note, however, that what is described in this chapter is not what will certainly happen, nor even what is very likely to happen, but what will happen to the parish, *if the premises of this volume are taken seriously.* One is permitted to be somewhat skeptical about the fulfillment of that condition.

First of all, there will be no single model for the parish of the future. Some parishes will be territorial, some will be "personal" (for specific groups, like professional people, business people, etc.), some will be large, though divided and sub-divided, and others will be small. Some parishes may put heavy emphasis on religious education, while others may stress social action, and still others will have a comprehensive liturgical program. The important point is that membership in a given parish will be optional, and no one will be automatically considered a member of a parish simply because he lives within its boundaries.

Catholics will be able to "shop" for the kind of parish that is most appropriate to their religious needs and desires, and (presumably through the clergy) will be permitted to engage in that kind of parochial work which matches their own talents and inclinations. Obviously, such a system will involve a certain confusion and uncertainty, but it will also produce much more vitality than the present extremely rigid division of the dioceses into territorial parishes.

The parish governance will be democratic, or if that word is too strong, at least collegial. The lay leadership of the parish will be elected, and we would not want to exclude the possibility of an election of clerical leadership, also. The making of broad general policy within a parish will be by consensus of the laity, religious, and clergy who constitute the parish. The implementation of decisions will also be on a collegial and consensual basis, involving either the whole parish in broad, practical decisions, or specific groups in matters which are their own proper concern. The status distinctions between clergy and laity will be less sharp. While it will be clear that the priest presides over the Eucharistic assembly, his role will neither isolate him from his people nor give him special decision-making prerogatives beyond his carefully defined powers as President of the collegial body.

The parish of the future will, certainly, have a profound liturgical life, which implies a liturgy geared to its own particular needs, celebrated at the most appropriate times, and in the format that responds to its own particular problems and aspirations. No worshiping congregation, at a given service, will be larger than will permit meaningful fellowship. If the parish is large, therefore, its ordinary worship will be decentralized and divided for the sub-communities within it, with only occasional calling together of all sub-communities in the "cathedral" type worship. The liturgy will be celebrated with dignity and reverence in the full realization that symbols are greatly important to worship. How far liturgical ceremonies will move in the direction of "low Church" or "high Church" will depend on the decisions and needs of the particular worshiping community.

The parish of the future will be primarily and essentially a community or, at least, a community of communities. It will stress the need for intimate and supportive primordial ties among the members of the congregation. There will be a marked familial spirit in the parish of the future, though how intimate the relationships among the parishioners are to be will depend upon the tastes and decisions of the members themselves. No a priori plan will force them to organize in a preconceived, rationalized way. Spontaneity and vitality will make for authentic community relations. Broad guidelines may be set down as to what constitutes a Christian community, but within these guidelines the nature of the familial and communitarian relationships will be dependent upon the decisions of the parishioners themselves.

The parish of the future, however, will not be an end in itself, but rather a service-oriented community, keenly aware that it assembles for the larger end of serving the Church and the city. The joy of common worship, the warmth of social support, the independence of collegial decision-making, a marked degree of freedom and flexibility—all these will promote its religious welfare. But that welfare itself will, we repeat, facilitate service to both

Church and city. Openness to that service will be, in fact, one of the essential characteristics of the future parish. Indeed, if it is merely parochial, it will not be considered genuinely Christian.

Furthermore, while considerable flexibility and self-direction will mark the parish of the future, it must realize that it is a sub-division of the diocese and that the local "church" of which it is part is the diocesan church. Therefore, the parish must be loyal to the diocese and must not see its welfare as something that can be isolated from that of the rest of the Church. Just as the bishop of the diocese must consider himself responsible for the welfare of the Church, so each parish community within the diocese must consider itself responsible for the whole diocese. It cannot feel that it has discharged its own obligation when it has provided for the religious needs of only its own members; it must rather consider its primary obligation to do all in its power to meet the religious and the human needs of the whole diocese.

The parish of the future will be functional in its organization. Its institutions and structures will persist as long as they serve some useful purpose in the achievement of the parish goals, and they will be eliminated when they become unnecessary. Instead of the formalized parish societies of the past, the parish of the future will be more likely to form *ad hoc* groups for specific purposes, dissolving them when these specific purposes are achieved. Some parish functions, such as teenage work, for example, presumably will be more permanent than others, but it is difficult to see how the parish of the future will have any need for organizations such as the Women's Society or the Men's Society. One would be inclined to think, as a matter of fact, that the CFM and the YCS (or their successors) will be typical of whatever permanent organizations the parish will sponsor.

Finally, the parish of the future will require distinctly less real estate. If the parents of the parish wish to send their children to Catholic schools, these schools will be administered largely by the diocese and local community school boards, which will be responsible for finances. The parish as such and its clergy will not be saddled with the responsibility of building, financing and maintaining the schools. Several parishes may well share the same school facilities under the direction of a school board independent of the parishes themselves (but appointed by the members of the parish). Existing parochial churches will not, of course, be torn down, but new churches, if indeed they are to be constructed, are likely to be much more modest in size and perhaps more artistic in design. Not all parishes, however, will need a church building, or be required to have one.

The parish of the future, therefore, will be more democratic, more liturgical, more communitarian, more flexible, more service-oriented, more functional in its organization and, probably, less encumbered with large physical facilities. It will be more mobile, able to act more quickly and change more rapidly. It will have greater resiliency—changing neighborhood conditions will not be the disaster for the parish that they frequently are now. It will be, at least in its highest manifestations, a parish capable of maintaining continuity with ecclesiastical tradition and, at the same time, quite skillful at "hanging loose" and "playing it by ear."

The parish of the future, as described in the perspective of sociology, has much in common with the parish as described in the Scriptures. It will consciously and deliberately strive to avoid becoming so rigid and inflexible in its organizational structure that it adjusts only very slowly to change. The essential difference between the parish of the present and the parish of the future is that the former—however unconsciously—is a means which has become an end, while the latter will be fully aware that it is a means to a larger end, and will attempt to incorporate into its life certain mechanisms which inhibit it from converting itself into an end.

The parish is perhaps the example par excellence of this phenomenon. Sociological theorists have used various terms for it, but the phenomenon is basically the same. Someone conceives a splendid idea and persuades his fellows to join him in the pursuit of the goal embodied in it. As more people are attracted to join the pursuit, it becomes necessary to organize them and to work out a clear division of labor. Soon the organization becomes formalized and routinized, and requires more and more effort for the maintenance of its own machinery, leaving less time and energy available for the pursuit of the goal which inspired it. The organization becomes more complex and elaborate, and its internal goals become more demanding. At last, the organization itself becomes the end, and the goal for which it was established is forgotten, unless for periodic ritualized justification of the organization's existence. In fact, the organization has now become self-justifying and the energies of its administrators are devoted almost entirely to its perpetuation, gradually frustrating the end for which it was established (as cited in Chapter V, this phenomenon has been aptly styled "The Iron Law of Oligarchy").

Thus, a parish, as a sub-division of the diocese, is founded both to provide worship at the local level *and* to serve the needs of the whole diocese. But with the passage of time, it largely ceases to exist for the diocese or for the service of the entire Church; it exists for itself, and the major concern of pastor and people alike become the preservation of the parish.

There are many other examples. The parish school was created to provide for the religious formation and education of the young people in the parish, but the maintenance of the school, in time, becomes an end in itself. No one feels impelled to reconsider what the school actually does or why it exists. Again, the offices of Pastor and Assistant were meant to provide wider service to growing parochial communities; although this relationship is clearly no longer of much service to the Church, it has become self-justifying, and so continues.

Ecclesiastical celibacy is another example. It developed in the Western Church for several reasons which have either ceased or have been lost sight of, but celibacy is justified by many simply on the grounds that it has so long existed. Any attempt to question, without prejudice, whether it is functional or dysfunctional for the Church at the present time is taken as a sign of dangerous radicalism.

Religious Orders are a further instance. They came into being for certain highly specific apostolic goals. But these goals, in many instances, have either been achieved or have been completely lost sight of. Nonetheless, self-preservation of the Order has become of such absolute importance to the leadership, and demands so much of their time, that they have little opportunity to ask whether the original goals of the community are being served, or whether the present organization of the community makes it possible for the community to achieve its orginal goals, or, indeed, any goal *outside itself.*

Again, parochial organizations were set up to promote public reverence for the name of the Lord, or to provide for the care of the altar. But now such societies are sacred in themselves, even though they no longer serve their original functions, and do not in fact attract very many members. Or, the Rule of Religious Communities and many of the provisions of Canon Law at one time were means to realistic ends, but at the present time they tend to find much of their justification within themselves, whether or not they are relevant to the problems of the Church and its members in the modern world. Yet, to question these is to risk being labeled a dangerous reformer.

Some older sociologists would have pronounced this process of "institutionalization" quite inevitable. In the view of the Jesuit ecumenist, Gustave Weigel, "all human enterprises, given sufficient time, go badly." The noted sociologist of religion, Thomas O'Dea, also held that institutionalization is inevitable and that it is bad.

But more recent writers are inclined to take a somewhat

different view. They argue that the evolution of complex institutions and elaborate bureaucracies *need not* destroy the vitality or the spontaneity of institutions, and that, on the contrary, institutions are absolutely necessary to social progress beyond primitive levels.

The author holds this latter position. Complex and elaborate organizations enable man to perform more tasks more effectively, to better develop his talents, and to bring to bear on the solution of his problems our collective human resources, skills and insights. For example, the Ford Motor Company today is, in its collectivity, both more productive *and more creative* than was the handful of people who started working in its founder's garage. Institutionalization, far from being an unmitigated evil, is an ambiguous development, bringing with it benefits that are fruitful and necessary, as well as dangers which are serious and threatening. The proper response to institutionalization is not to denounce it, as some sociologists do, or to attempt to eliminate it, as some naive reformers propose. The sophisticated and intelligent approach to institutionalization is to realize that it is a phenomenon with which man must live, and to build into institutions those mechanisms which will maximize benefits, while minimizing dangers.

At least three such "mechanisms" are especially relevant to the parish of the future, as well as to the Church of the future. First of all, as stated before, it is necessary that its staff (and here we mean, particularly, the clergy and other professional or religious functionaries) possess a high degree of internalized motivation—plus enough personal security to allow for innovation and creativity, and freedom to act on their own initiative and responsibility. Secondly, no matter how complex or sophisticated the institution becomes, it must realize that essential to effectiveness is the maintenance of healthy friendship groups among its members, and that these groups will function effectively only when they *are* given maximum freedom and responsibility. Thirdly, the institution must make sure that it is capable of systematic self-criticism. Unless it includes an agency for internal self-criticism, a complex institution or even a relatively uncomplex one like the parish of the future, can easily grow complacent and stagnant. One of the great weaknesses of most modern parishes is that its leader is usually sheltered from unfavorable comment, by his assistants and his people, and one of the major obstacles to the new openness of communication in the Church is this: men who have been sheltered from criticism find it very difficult to cope with, when it is finally offered. In the parish of the future, parochial leaders will be eager for honest criticism because they will realize that without it they will simply lose all real effectiveness.

In such a perspective, the task for the parish and the Church is not to eliminate institutionalism but to achieve such professionalism, decentralization, and honest criticism within the institution that these built-in features will continually revitalize it.

It may be argued that the parish of the future which we here describe is a dreamer's utopian parish. And certainly there are not many such parishes now, nor are there likely to be many in the foreseeable future. But because we do not have them and do not seem to be in the process of developing them, it does not follow that they are either theoretically or practically impossible. It simply means that we do not have the wisdom and the courage necessary to create them. Until we do, sociologists must find few organizations in the world where the Iron Law of Oligarchy operates as infallibly as it does in the Catholic Church.

But wisdom and courage have defied such laws before now. And when these virtues burst upon the world, quite indiscriminately and unpredictably, as they did in the unpretentious old man revered as John XXIII, the event is something more than mere history. It assumes the proportions of an exception to the law, in favor of life and renewal.

15 Leadership
and the Christian Community

American Catholicism is, I think, coming to the end of an
era which has viewed leadership with suspicion and distrust, and the leadership of the hierarchy as really quite
unnecessary in the Church (even as many priests have con-
tended vigorously that their role as "president of the
eucharistic community" involves no leadership functions
beyond presiding over the celebration of the Eucharist).
For it has not taken very long for most Catholics to realize
that "leaderless" communities shortly cease to exist as
communities. Furthermore, the social scientific concept of
leadership does have the extraordinary merit of demonstrating that a genuinely "democratic" leader exercises
more power rather than less.[1] Thus, the concept of democratic authority becomes an extremely useful standard
with which to measure the functioning of leadership in the
Church.

[1] See Chapters 6 and 7 of my book, *The Hesitant Pilgrim* (New York:
Sheed & Ward, 1966), pp. 61-117.

Unfortunately, naive and oversimplified interpretations of the "group dynamics" concept of leadership can corrupt this model as much as the notion of "community" has been corrupted. I would like to suggest, therefore, that the work of Provost Warren G. Bennis, of the State University of New York at Buffalo be made required reading for every Catholic, cleric or lay, who proposes to talk about "leadership," at least in the decade ahead. And I would particularly recommend Chapter 5, "New Patterns of Leadership for Adaptive Organizations" in Provost Bennis's book, *The Temporary Society*. I might note for those "sensitivity training" enthusiasts who never bother to read the literature on their new passion, that Mr. Bennis's credentials in this area are impeccable.

He prescribes six main tasks for leadership in an adaptive organization:

1. *Integration.* By this he means a system of "rewards" within an organization which makes possible the satisfactory personal and professional growth of its members. The leader must be sure that there are enough basic human satisfactions within his organization to keep it operating effectively.

2. *Social influence.* By this Bennis means that a leader must develop "executive constellations," and he observes:

> It is quaint to think that one man, no matter how omniscient and omnipotent, can comprehend, to say nothing of control, the diversity and complexity of the modern organization. Followers and leaders who think this is possible get entrapped in a false dream, a

child's fantasy of absolute power and absolute dependence.[2]

The leader, then, must put together a team of people who will combine the skills, insights, and enthusiasm necessary to operate the organization effectively. He cannot do it by himself, nor with one or two cronies, nor with a group of incompetent mediocrities.

3. *Collaboration.* In addition to bringing together the "executive constellation," the leader must create a climate in which the members of the team are motivated to co-operate effectively with one another. Such a climate, according to Bennis, includes the following ingredients:

> . . . flexible and adaptive structure, utilization of member talents, clear and agreed upon goals, norms of openness, trust, and cooperation, inner-dependence, high intrinsic rewards and transactional controls, i.e., members of the unit should have a high degree of autonomy and a high degree of participation in making key decisions.[3]

Bennis calls this collaborative effort "synergy," and he points out that it is extremely hard to develop:

> Lack of experience and strong cultural biases against group efforts worsen the problem. Groups, like other

[2] Warren G. Bennis and P. E. Slater, *The Temporary Society* (New York: Harper & Row, 1968), pp. 103-104.
[3] *Op. cit.,* p. 105.

highly complicated organisms, need time to develop. They require time, interaction, trust, communication, and commitment, and these ingredients require a period of gestation. I am as continually amazed at expectation of easy maturity in groups as I would be in young children.[4]

4. *Adaptation*. Bennis notes that any modern organization is going to be faced with the problem of constant change, and that the leadership must learn how to "roll with" the change, neither resisting change for the sake of resistance nor accepting change for the sake of change:

Modern organizations, even more than individuals, are acutely vulnerable to the problem of responding flexibly and appropriately to new information. Symptoms of maladaptive responses, at the extremes are (1) a guarded, frozen, rigid response, denying the presence or avoiding the recognition of changes, resulting most typically in organizational paralysis; or (2) susceptibility to change resulting in a spastic, unreliable faddism. It is obvious that there are times when openness to change is appropriate and other times when it may be disastrous. Organizations, in fact, should reward people who act as counterchange agents, creating forces against the seduction of newness for its own sake.[5]

[4] *Op. cit.*, p. 106.
[5] *Op. cit.*, pp. 107-108.

Good leadership, then, creates a climate with enough security to change and enough resistance to avoid precipitate change: "Creating an environment that would increase a tolerance for ambiguity and where one can make a virtue out of uncertainty, rather than one that induces hesitancy and its reckless counterpart, expediency, is one of the most challenging tasks for new leadership."[6]

5. *Identity.* Organizations, Bennis says, like individuals, suffer from identity crisis, a point which hardly needs to be made with regard to American Catholicism at the present time. The critical role of the leader is to keep clear in his own mind and in the mind of his associates what the common goals are, so that the organization does not become like the modern university which, as Robert Hutchins once said, is held together by a central heating system, or in Clark Kerr's more recent version, by a common parking problem. It is so very easy for human beings to become involved in their own particular problems that they forget the common goal which has brought them together in an organization. If leadership permits itself to be bogged down in its own administrative difficulties and ignores the "big picture," it had better find some functional equivalent of a parking problem, lest the organization disintegrate completely! One might also add that in an organization like the Church, whose supra-organizational goals are so vast and immense, the *prophetic* role of the leader—to keep the goals clearly before the minds of his followers—is an extremely important one.

6. *Revitalization.* An organization either controls its

6 *Op. cit.,* pp. 108-109.

own destiny or yields itself to the massive social and cultural forces that swirl around it. Bennis's words on the subject serve as a perfect description of the problems of the contemporary Church:

> For the leader, revitalization means that the organization has to take a conscious responsibility for its own evolution; that without a planned methodology and explicit direction the enterprise will not realize its full potential. For the leader the issue of revitalization confronts him with the penultimate challenge—growth or decay. The challenge for the leader is to develop a climate of inquiry and enough psychological and employment security for continued reassessment and renewal.[7]

This description of the leadership role can be fruitfully considered as an abstract analysis of the behavior of the most effective leaders of the modern world—men like John XXIII and President Kennedy—and ought to provide an extraordinarily useful tool for reevaluating the role of leadership in the Church. It does not imply that leaders are less important, but rather that they are more important. It does not indicate that we must abolish leadership, but rather that we must renovate and reinvigorate it. But—and the *but* is an important one—the naive enthusiast who thinks that one sensitivity training experience tells him all there is to know about modern leadership will be even more of a liability to the Church than is the ingenuous enthusiast for community.

[7] *Op. cit.*, p. 112.

Another contribution the social scientist can make in the contemporary Church is the conduct of research, that is, the clarification of problems and the investigation of a range of alternative responses. Here, I must confess, I find myself quite pessimistic. The Catholic Church in the United States has yet to spend even remotely adequate sums of money on a single important research project. And while "surveys," "self-studies," "polls," and "projects" abound, almost all of them tend to be of the amateur and bargain-basement variety. Some of these efforts have proven incredibly good, others are unbelievably bad. But none of them represents as yet, an adequate or systematic response by American Catholicism to the potential value of social science research.

For example, at the present time the National Conference of Catholic Bishops is apparently prepared to embark on a major survey of the priesthood, a survey in which the present writer and a number of his colleagues are to be involved. But, for my part, I must confess considerable ambivalence about the prospects of such a project.

My ambivalence is not about the utility of the project, nor whether it will be done with professional competence. My doubts, rather, are whether it will make any difference, for there is no point in investing large sums of money in careful and professional research if there does not exist a climate in which such research will be accepted for what it is—the clarification of issues and the specification of alternative responses. Father William Rooney, of the Catholic Commission on Intellectual and Cultural Affairs, has long insisted on the need to develop a climate of respect for research and learning among American Catholics. But despite the great progress that has been made in the last decade, I am not sure that behavioral science research will be accepted by either the right or the left wing of American Catholicism.

Thus, the proposed survey of the Catholic priesthood begins, I think, under very awkward circumstances. Various Catholic liberal journals have already suggested that the research is unnecessary, too expensive, and biased. Also, one is not at all sure whether the ecclesiastical leadership itself is prepared to accept the research when it is finished. Admittedly, the project was unanimously endorsed by the National Conference of Catholic Bishops, but a letter sent to all the priests in the country by the committee which is sponsoring it managed to get buried in the basements of most of the chancery offices of the large archdioceses—including my own. Apparently, the project is either too unimportant, or too dangerous for the notice of the priests of the country. In any case, there is little reason to hope that the project will be accepted when it is completed.

Thus, American Catholicism at present is enthusiastic about "quick," "simple," and "inexpensive" surveys and self-studies, but profoundly skeptical about professional and careful research. There are, of course, many exceptions to this generalization, including, I must say, the bishops who are serving together with the priest scholars on the NCCB's Commission for the Study of the Life and Ministry of the Priest. But exceptions do not establish a climate, and I cannot honestly report that the climate for serious pastoral research in the United States is good at the present time.

Reluctantly, I must conclude this book by observing that the several major contributions social science can make to the Church are neither accepted or understood within American Catholicism at large. When sociology attempts realistically to consider the limitations on pastoral activity, it is dismissed as tired and pessimistic. When it attempts to insist on precision in the use of sociological models for reviewing and interpreting reality, it is dismissed as imperalistic and "academic." Finally, when it attempts to do careful and precise research, it is either ignored or condemned as biased. Any other assessment of the situation would, in my judgment, be at variance with the facts. Sociology is tossed into the crucible of change, all right, but I fear it is either expected to work some instant alchemy, or it is regarded as a mere catalytic agent.

Yet there are reasons, I think, to be hopeful. The cadre of trained social scientists in American Catholicism is increasing, as is the number of ecclesiastical administrators who understand what social research is, and who know both what it can do and what it cannot do. Furthermore, the number of such administrators who insist absolutely that all research be conducted competently and professionally is increasing. My own personal hunch is that the more serious problem in the future will not be with the administrators, but with the rank and file of the clergy and the concerned laity, who expect quick and magic answers. But it does seem to me that the younger generation of clergy and laity, with much better social science training in their own educational experience, envince both a healthy respect and a healthy skepticism toward social science. The sociologist can ask no more.

I would conclude, therefore, that while the era of responsible and intelligent "pastoral sociology" is not yet born, it may be aborning. And this means hope, because while sociologists certainly are quite incapable of resolving the problems that the Catholic Church faces in the modern world, they have, I think, an important contribution to make toward the solution of such problems. It would be unfortunate if this contribution were to be ignored. However modest and limited, it offers many proven aids for reconstructing the Church of God's people.